A Brighter Blueprint

The Twelve Threads of Effective Advocacy

Lesa Brackbill

Library of Congress Control Number: 2026905935

ISBNs:
979-8-218-93808-6 (Paperback)
979-8-218-93809-3 (Hardcover)
979-8-295-62676-0 (eBook)

Book Cover and Illustrations by Dan Deming-Henes, *Stranded Design Co.*
Author Photo by Sarah Benner, *Perigee Photo Co.*
Contributions by Mike Walsh and Josh Argall
Editing by Kari Livesay

Interior photographs by the author unless otherwise indicated.

Published by Patient Advocacy Strategies
https://brighterblueprint.patientadvocacystrategies.com

First Edition: 2026

Printed in the United States of America

Contents

For Victoria, whose legacy is the light in every thread.

For Isaiah and Caleb, who remind me why we keep weaving.

*And for all who know that it doesn't have to be this way—
and are brave enough to change it.*

Foreword
By Nicole Guysi

I was thrust into advocacy as a child, feeling deeply that the environments I found myself in were not right, yet my voice was often silenced and dismissed. At that time, I didn't know how to advocate. When you find yourself in survival mode, advocacy is not always something you can prioritize. There was no blueprint for me, only examples of what I knew I did not want to follow, and my youthful attempts to make myself heard, known, and safe. It took many years, numerous failures, misunderstandings, and hard lessons to learn many of the things that Lesa has so effectively laid out for her readers.

I imagine many of us have entertained the idea of writing a book. For those who have allowed that thought to linger, I wonder if we have all thought, "Surely this book already exists?" A friend affectionately labeled me a bibliophile; my bookshelf is overflowing with fiction of all kinds and a variety of non-fiction categories, including adulting, Christianity, leadership, and more. So when Lesa asked for readers to provide authentic feedback on her new book, I was eager to participate for multiple reasons!

Of course, one reason was simply the opportunity to read something new, which I always jump on. The main reason, however, was that while Lesa and I have advocated alongside each other, we have also had private, thoughtful discussions. We met through a Newborn Screening Ambassadors group, and I have felt blessed that our paths crossed since that day. I wouldn't say we always agree, but we can articulate our viewpoints while recognizing that there may be more to the discussion than what either of us initially perceives. Instead of making assumptions, we engage in dialogue, not to persuade but to understand each other while clearly conveying our own perspectives. As you can imagine, this is a valuable advocacy skill. So when I heard that she had written a blueprint, I was eager to read it.

What you will find in this blueprint is nothing short of extraordinary. There is a wealth of curriculum available on advocacy, presenters, and programs, each serving its purpose. I highly recommend that anyone in any stage of their advocacy journey explore these resources. However, I have yet to see a comprehensive plan made available to such a broad audience.

As I mentioned earlier, my advocacy journey began in childhood. My negative experiences led me to overreact, which often put me in a "fight mode" rather than a true advocacy mindset. Lesa understands that many of us who feel beaten down, unheard, or undervalued share this inclination. What she has created is a plan that can (and should) be executed by anyone, presented in a way that is as comforting as a weighted blanket paired with your favorite book.

Lesa draws upon her past and current personal and professional experiences, delivering them in a manner that almost any learning style can grasp. I will admit that I struggle to comprehend concepts I have never personally experienced. I tend to read materials in order, going through them completely, but if I can't relate to the content, my reading becomes superficial. Lesa seems to have designed her chapters with readers like me in mind. Even if I unintentionally overlook certain sections, the songs she introduces, the movies she references, and the colorful charts and exercises interspersed throughout the chapters allow me to engage deeply with the robust information they contain. I find myself relating her examples to my own past experiences or seeing how they apply to the current climate of our community.

This book is written from the heartfelt passion of a beautiful soul eager to share her lessons and discoveries. Because it stems from both courage and humility, I hope this blueprint reaches all future advocates and those currently advocating in any capacity.

This isn't just a guide for effective advocacy; it represents how advocacy should be done, period.

I encourage you to start a playlist, grab a notebook and writing utensils, and gather any coloring tools that inspire you. This book is designed to be marked up, written in, learned from, and acted upon. It aims to challenge you, challenge existing systems, and be challenged itself.

Don't let the author, the content, or the examples intimidate you. You can apply this blueprint to anything from advocating over the phone for an insurance bill to lobbying on Capitol Hill, and everything in between.

While the book is versatile, there will inevitably be situations it doesn't cover. I encourage you to reflect on why those instances don't fit and either adjust your perspective or accept that the book may not address them... yet. I've already suggested to Lesa that given the evolving nature of advocacy, a second edition may be needed at some point.

We enter advocacy for various reasons and experience different seasons throughout our journeys. This blueprint will equip you, regardless of your level of experience. There are many lessons to be learned from this book, but I want to leave you with this important thought: while this book can enhance your advocacy skills, I boldly assert that improving your advocacy is not its primary intent.

If you apply this blueprint, your advocacy will sharpen—that's great for you. However, the true value lies in what that improvement will accomplish. When advocates possess humility, competence, enhanced knowledge, and improved skills, the real outcomes become apparent: awareness is raised, systems are refined, and ultimately, lives are improved and, in some cases, saved.

This is the essence of quality advocacy, and this blueprint is your path to achieving it.

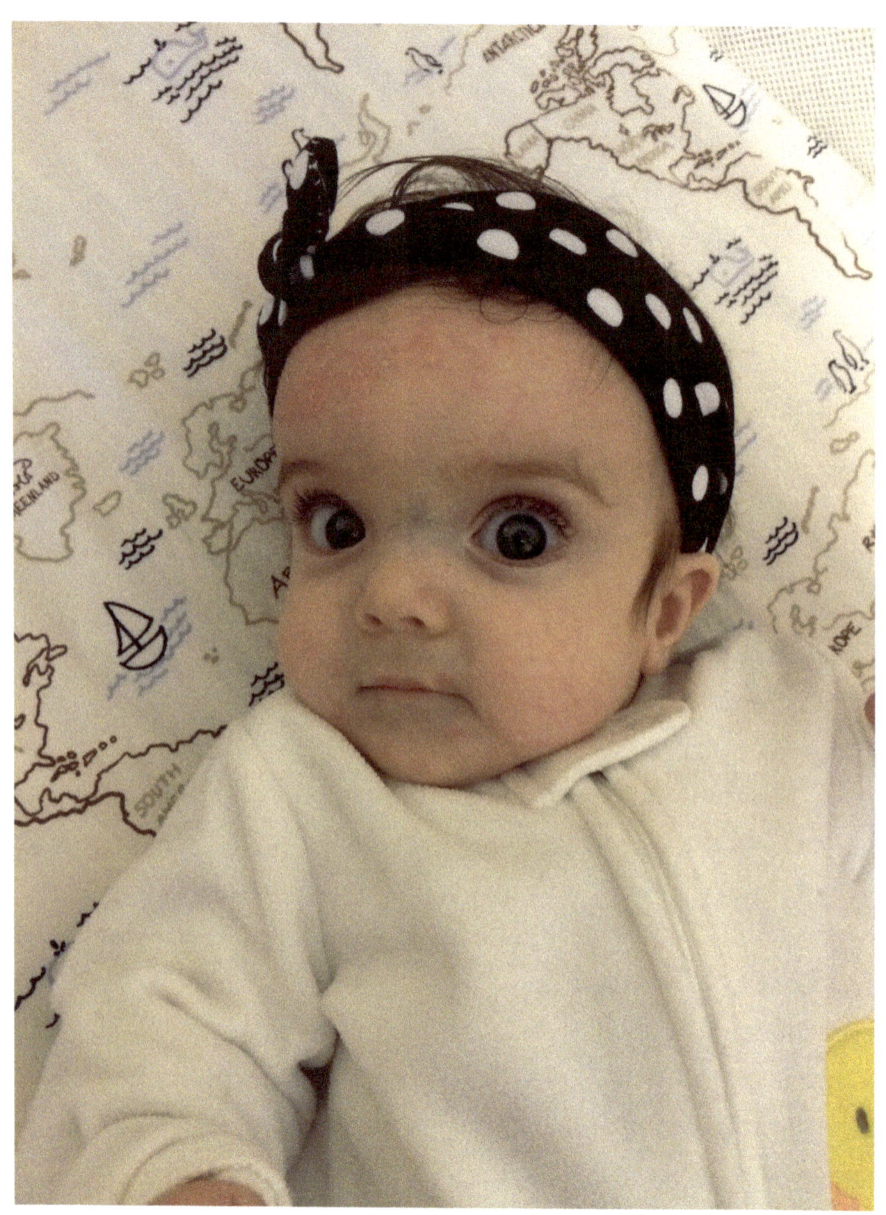

Preface
Weaving Purpose From Pain

My husband and I both agree that Friday, February 13, 2015, was the worst day of our lives. We had endured a six-week diagnostic odyssey for our infant daughter, Victoria. The full weight of our dread settled in a dull exam room with beige walls, where a neurologist gently spoke the two most devastating words we could have heard:

"It's Krabbe."

Our six-month-old daughter was dying.

When we pressed her for options, pleading for something—anything—we could try, she uttered the words that haunt me still:

"If you had caught it at birth, you could have treated it."

In that moment, the various threads of my life—my political science degree, my lobbying experience, and my passion for helping others—suddenly snapped into a single, devastating focus. I couldn't deny that this was always supposed to be my story, even though I would do anything to change it. I went from being a first-time parent desperate to love my child to a parent desperate to re-engineer a broken system. I could not save Tori, but I could fix the machinery that failed her. I had no idea where to start, but I knew I had to take action.

Before I began, however, my husband and I made a decision: we would cherish the time we had with Tori while she was alive. We completed fifty *Bucket List* adventures, all while learning to be caregivers and managing a household filled with medical equipment. We chose joy during a time when it would have been easier to succumb to grief.

Our adventures with Tori were about more than simply making memories; we were finding light in the darkness. This lesson became a core part of my advocacy: **grief fuels the work, but joy sustains it.**

Knowing the Why

I know more about Krabbe disease than I know about my daughter, Tori.

I will never know Tori's favorite color, food, or song. I will never get to hear her talk about anything or say "mama."

My knowledge of my precious daughter is painfully limited.

Being in the rare disease community is a delicate balance of beauty and pain. Every one of us is on a journey that no one would have chosen. We are all grieving in our own way—grieving the present and the future, mourning what could have been. Many of us feel compelled to make a positive impact on the world because of everything we've endured; I certainly do. There's a deep desire to create a legacy for our child or loved one since they cannot do so themselves.

While I may not know if Tori liked giraffes, I do know the pain of Krabbe disease and the agony of not having the chance to save my child. I don't want others to face the same path we did. I want them to have options and to hold onto hope.

My lack of knowledge about Tori, combined with the trauma I experienced and the loss I endured, motivates me to create a lifetime of memories for others—easing their burden and offering new possibilities. This is the *why* that drives me forward daily, both personally and professionally.

I may not know your personal *why,* but I'm grateful to have you alongside me on this journey.

Dreams and Learning Curves

Every first-time parent has dreams for their child, filled with a sense of wonder at this new life and excitement about the child's limitless potential. Parents may imagine what their child will become and the impact they might have on the world. Perhaps they even consider the legacy their child will create—I know we certainly did. What we didn't expect was that we would be the ones to create it.

When Tori was diagnosed with Krabbe disease, I felt utterly helpless. Her diagnosis came too late for treatment, and all we could do was wait.

New parents are supposed to think about the life the child will live, not how or when they will die. Yet for most of Tori's life, we were forced to ponder her death.

After her death, fourteen months post-diagnosis, I began advocating for expanded newborn screening, driven by a deep sense of urgency to spare others the suffering we endured. I realized that my work would be her legacy, so I set out to build it.

However, that doesn't mean I had it all figured out.

What I Wish I'd Known Before I Started

Here are a few lessons I learned along the way that may help you.

Take time to heal: After a diagnosis or a loss, it's natural to feel a sense of urgency. The impulse to jump right into advocacy is understandable, but it's crucial to prioritize your family's well-being and mental health. There will always be time to add your voice. Don't let distractions replace your grief—take the time to work through it.

It's okay to wait: I'm grateful I waited to begin my advocacy work until after my daughter had passed away. Every situation is different, and you have the power to wait until the moment is right for YOU. We chose to cherish every moment with Tori while she was still here; I knew that focusing on advocacy would distract me from the precious few months we had left. No one will judge you for choosing time with your loved one.

Know yourself: Recognize your triggers for grief, anxiety, or whatever your situation may be. Know when to advocate and when to rest. It's perfectly okay to say, "not this time" when asked to speak or participate in something. Learning about myself has been one of the hardest lessons, but prioritizing my health and well-being must come first.

Grief can be blinding: If your advocacy stems from personal loss, be mindful of how grief can affect your perspective. It's easy to assume the worst about others and to misinterpret your painful feelings as objective reality. Recognizing this allows you to step back and respond strategically rather than react emotionally.

You don't have to have it all figured out to get started: I eventually built a team through individual conversations that guided me in changing policy in Pennsylvania. Fear can arise from not knowing what to do; take it step by step and one conversation at a time, building your courage along the way. No one expects you to be perfect, even though you may expect it from yourself. Your presence and effort will foster your courage and, in turn, inspire others.

The Invitation

This book is not a memoir of loss; it is a practical guide for advocates ready to move from awareness to action.

These *Twelve Threads* are not quick fixes; they are significant and, at times, challenging. They require a *growth mindset* that embraces discomfort. Throughout my life, I have realized that growth and ease rarely coexist. The discomfort signifies the expansion of your perspective. If a thread feels difficult to weave—if it's challenging to listen to a critic or remain nonpartisan—that's simply the sound of the tapestry becoming stronger. Growth occurs in discomfort.[1]

I may not know your personal *why*, but I understand the weight of the burden you carry. I want to help you create a blueprint that holds, a system that works, and a legacy that lasts.

I am glad you're on this journey with me.

Your courage to speak up for others
inspires others to find their courage.

Mindy Summers

Introduction
The Power of Hope

Background Music: I Saw What I Saw (Sara Groves)

This song is the anthem of the unfinished task. Groves captures the exact moment when the comfort of ignorance is traded for the weight of responsibility. She sings, "I saw what I saw, and I can't forget it." This is the heartbeat of advocacy. Advocacy doesn't start with a law or a meeting; it starts with an observation that burns into your soul. Once you see the mess of the system, you have a choice: you can walk away, or you can pick up the shuttle and begin to weave something better. This song is the bridge between the grief of what is and the courage of what could be.

Honoring the Mess

I am not a weaver, but I have friends who have developed the skill and I am amazed at their craftsmanship. They can take spools of thread and create something beautiful, something useful. Some of them even shear the sheep themselves, make their own yarn, dye it, and then weave it. It takes hours of disciplined work, but the result is worth it.

Weaving is a universal language. Nearly every culture has its own method and style, expressing its history through creation. But what surprised me most as I learned about this craft was how messy the back of a woven object can look at times. If you look at the underside of a masterpiece, you might see a chaotic nest of knots, loose ends, and crossing lines. It is difficult to imagine the beauty on the other side when you are looking at the tangles.

This is the perfect metaphor for advocacy.

Front and back of a Tunisian woven rug

I often feel like the back of a tapestry. This book reveals the messiness I have endured while learning to advocate effectively—it's the book I wish I'd had ten years ago. I knew what I wanted to achieve, but I lacked a pattern or blueprint to help me get there.

In the advocacy space, we engage with diverse personalities, conflicting objectives, and varying life experiences. We have goals we want to achieve, but without clear direction and dedication, they will never come to fruition. The threads may appear messy from the back.

Advocacy is the act of taking those tangled threads on the "back end" and persistently weaving them together until a clear, functional pattern emerges on the front.

If your work feels like a tangle of loose ends right now, don't panic—that means you are working on the back end of something beautiful. The most beautiful tapestries are woven from the threads of our hardest seasons.

The Brighter Blueprint

This book's idea originated from a simple question:
What makes an advocate effective?

Even after more than ten years in advocacy, I hadn't fully considered what drives effectiveness until my friend, Sarah Cortell Vandersypen, posed that question as we prepared for a conference. This question led me to reflect, observe, and research. The initial presentation evolved into blog posts, and now, this book.

While people and organizations often create plans and objectives—a blueprint—these tend to be flat and two-dimensional. Effective advocacy, however, resembles weaving a tapestry where each thread represents vital skills and diverse voices on this journey. It creates a rich fabric imbued with the texture of strategic action and ethical values.

This book provides a *Brighter Blueprint* as a guiding framework: a set of *Twelve Threads* designed to help you transition from merely battling the system to becoming a master weaver who shapes a resilient and just solution. Don't be overwhelmed by the number of threads; you will quickly see the significance of each one and how its impact expands when connected to others. If we are willing to weave them together, this blueprint can transform into a beautiful tapestry.

Ultimately, the *Brighter Blueprint* serves as a guide for anyone ready to stop fighting against the system and start re-engineering it to be more equitable, ethical, and effective for everyone. This book serves as the loom on which you can weave your own passion into a truly effective strategy.

Good Trouble

> Never, ever be afraid to make some noise
> and get in good trouble, necessary trouble.
>
> John Lewis

John Lewis was an inspiring man, and he was known for encouraging others to get into "good trouble."[1] Good trouble requires a great blueprint. Without a plan, good trouble is just noise. With a plan, good trouble is a catalyst.

To successfully get into "good trouble" while you navigate the marathon of advocacy, you must understand that you are operating at the intersection of art and science.

The **tapestry** represents the art. It embodies relationships, shared stories, and your lived experiences. It is soft, human, and colorful—the very elements that make people care. Without this artistic aspect, advocacy reduces to cold paperwork.

The **blueprint** represents the science. It illustrates the legislative process, raw data, budget cycles, and systemic obstacles. It is complex, structured, and technical—essential for making the mission work.

I have learned that while the languages of advocacy may change—from the earthquake rubble in Haiti to the marketplaces of Tunisia, and to the Pennsylvania Capitol—the mechanics of hope remain constant.

The *Brighter Blueprint* combines the clarity of an engineer's technical drawing with the vibrant, human colors of a weaver's tapestry. To change the world, one must possess the heart of a weaver to connect with people and the mind of an engineer to mend the broken system.

Common Ground

While writing this book and reviewing images from my personal collection, I discovered photographs of weaving from both Tunisia and Guatemala—two separate continents, an ocean apart, yet showcasing the same craft and similar threads.

We are all more similar than we tend to assume, and yet it's so easy to choose indifference over empathy.

At the core of the *Brighter Blueprint* lies a simple, ancient principle: **Love your neighbor.** In today's world, we often focus on our differing values and overlook the fact that our intrinsic needs and values are usually the same. We all desire safety for our children, dignity for our elders, and a system that supports us in our most vulnerable moments. You don't have to share a neighbor's political views to empathize with their challenges. Finding common ground is not about compromising your beliefs; it's about recognizing that the person across the table is also a weaver, striving to make sense of a complex world.

Advocacy is the intentional act of taking the discomfort of a broken reality and weaving it into a *Brighter Blueprint* for others.

Love in Unexpected Places (New Orleans, 2008)

Advocacy involves transforming from a victim of the system into its architect, choosing to exchange idealism for realism to build something that truly saves lives. We don't weave because the process is easy; we weave because every individual deserves to find a safety net awaiting them.

The Core Challenge

For many, the advocacy journey begins during a crisis. In the rare disease community, this is often marked by *Diagnosis Day*, which thrusts individuals into complex medical systems and deep grief. I've observed that many well-meaning advocates struggle to navigate public health and government systems, facing the same obstacles and burnout. Sometimes, they unintentionally harm the very systems they aim to improve. Advocacy is filled with passionate individuals who often make similar well-intentioned mistakes. I wrote this book to help make your journey easier and to help you avoid the missteps I have made along the way.

Ironically, for many of us, our advocacy efforts aim to eliminate our own roles. In rare disease, we work so that the name of our condition fades into history, becoming just a footnote in medical textbooks. We envision a future where quick diagnoses and effective treatments are standard in healthcare, reducing the need for continued advocacy because families and patients would no longer face the struggles and grief that are all too common today.

How can we turn this vision into reality?

We need a *Brighter Blueprint*.

Potholes, Skyscrapers, and the Loom

My advocacy journey began with a personal tragedy, but the mission was forged over the 2,292 days that followed. I spent more than six years navigating a complex public health bureaucracy and the labyrinth of the Pennsylvania legislature before achieving success. The lessons I learned—and the mistakes I still sometimes make—are woven into the pages of this book. Along the way, I discovered a vital truth:

The scale of your actions does not determine the depth of your impact.

In the world of change-making, we often focus on two extremes: potholes and skyscrapers. My goal is to guide you from a reactive, fragmented approach to an intentional, sustainable influence. This book isn't about being a perfect advocate; it's about being a *present* one.

The world needs your story, told in your own imperfect voice.

The Diagnostic Power of the Pothole

Potholes represent the daily friction within a system: a confusing form, a bottlenecked process, or a lapse in communication. We often overlook these issues, yet addressing small obstacles can create a ripple effect of benefits that are felt directly and personally. Repairing a pothole is usually more sustainable than enacting a new law because it becomes part of the established processes—essentially an administrative best practice.

I learned this lesson in the marketplaces of Chimaltenango, Guatemala. Later in this book, you will read about how purchasing avocados from a woman had a greater impact than we anticipated. Effective advocacy often emerges from these quiet, human-scale adjustments. When you fix a pothole so effectively that future generations are unaware that the problem ever existed, you have succeeded.

However, a pothole also serves as a diagnostic tool. If you identify the same crack in multiple locations, you haven't just found a nuisance; you have discovered a flaw in the very blueprint of the road itself and you may need a new plan to fix it.

The Illusion of the Skyscraper

Skyscrapers represent the grand, highly visible monuments to a cause—those landmark legislative victories we celebrate in the news. While essential, skyscrapers can be fragile and costly in terms of time, energy, and capital. Often, the law itself is seen as the win rather than the brokenness it repaired.

Too often, we construct these monuments while leaving the operational potholes unaddressed, resulting in an impressive structure that is unstable or inaccessible to the people it serves. A new administration can demolish a skyscraper, but it is much harder to reverse a process that has become the new standard. Addressing potholes is not a lesser form of advocacy; it is, in fact, the most sustainable approach.

Introducing the Twelve Threads

The shape of my work—from medical and policy advocacy to humanitarian work and my current role on a local school board—has always varied and the threads have different lengths, thicknesses, and colors. However, every endeavor has required these *Twelve Threads*, and I am excited to share these insights with you.

Core	The Thread	The Weaver's Manifesto
Setting the Anchor: Mindset & Character	Pink (Maintain Resilience)	I am resilient, sustainable, and grounded in the joy of the work
	White (Practice Humility)	I am a low-ego collaborator, ready to admit what I don't know.
	Silver (Bridge the Divide)	I am a nonpartisan bridge-builder; the mission is my only party.
Drafting the Pattern: Science of the System	Yellow (Learn & Unlearn)	I am evidence-based, curious, and committed to systemic truth.
	Blue (Listen for the Unspoken)	I hear the unspoken fears and priorities behind the resistance.
	Red (Speak with Integrity)	I am an unassailable advocate who speaks with clarity and integrity.
Mastering the Weave: Power of the Guild	Gold (Level the Loom)	I am a champion of equity who centers lived authority in every solution.
	Green (Forge Alliances)	I gather a coalition of partners to amplify our collective voice.
	Gray (Lead Ethically)	I am a trusted broker, guided by a moral North Star that does not shift.
	Orange (Share the Credit)	I give the credit away, ensuring our allies stay for the win.
Building the Momentum: Mechanics of Change	Brown (Act Strategically)	I execute the technical steps to fix the system.
	Purple (Master the Pivot)	I am strategically agile, letting new data dictate the direction of my turn

In the *Brighter Blueprint*, color carries weight. Every hue was selected to evoke the essence of its corresponding thread. In the chart above, you'll find each characteristic paired with a manifesto-style sentence detailing how it transforms the way we approach advocacy.

What to Expect

I wanted this book to feel like an experience, one that would keep the reader engaged and help convey these ideas in a variety of ways. To accomplish this, I included the following elements in each chapter:

The Rhythm of Advocacy

Advocacy work is rarely silent; it has its own rhythm. As a vocalist and musician, I have always understood the world through melody. Each of the *Twelve Threads* is paired with a song that captures its specific energy. At the end of the book, you'll find a QR code for a digital toolkit that also includes a link to my playlist, and I encourage you to create your own advocacy soundtrack as well.

The Narrative Lens

Knowledge is strengthened when it is witnessed. To help you identify these threads in the real world, each chapter includes a suggested film that acts as a case study for that specific thread. By viewing these threads through a narrative lens, you can integrate them more effectively into your own advocacy efforts and daily lives.

The Interlock: Strengthening the Weave

In each chapter, you will find a section dedicated to *The Interlock*. In weaving, a single thread can easily be pulled out or snapped. However, when threads interlock, they physically grip each other. They stop being mere individual strands and instead create a cohesive fabric. If you treat these *Twelve Threads* as isolated strands, your advocacy may be colorful but ultimately weak. To build a movement capable of withstanding systemic change, you must master *The Interlock*. The end of each chapter contains a chart of these interlocks specific to the color being discussed. These show you how to connect your values so your mission does not fray.

Thread Experiments

For each thread, you'll find a suggested activity or action to help you see the thread in practice. Occasionally, I'll include bonus ideas to reinforce the key concepts of each thread. These are not meant to add to your already long to-do list; instead, they are designed to offer different ways to solidify your understanding of the ideas in a manner that resonates with you as the reader. Do them, don't do them—it's entirely up to you. They are there if you're up for a little bit of adventure.

The Power of Hope

When we experience a significant loss or setback and things feel out of control, we choose how we respond. There are no right or wrong answers, and no strict timelines. However, I hope you will choose hope.

> **Hope has two beautiful daughters;**
> **their names are Anger and Courage.**
> **Anger at the way things are,**
> **and Courage to see that they do not remain as they are.**
> Attributed to Saint Augustine

Hope can be both a noun and a verb. It encompasses two powerful forces: anger at injustice and the courage to take action. Although it can be excruciating at times, hope inspires us to act and drives us toward the future we seek. This book provides the tools, language, and strategies you need to channel your hope, anger, and courage into concrete and impactful advocacy efforts. May you choose hope as we work together to address the injustices in our world.

Welcome to the loom. Let's begin to weave.

Defining Advocacy
It's Not Just Politics

The Race We Run

Advocacy is often misunderstood as something that only occurs within the walls of a Capitol building. While it may seem like a big word that carries a heavy weight, it's essential to know that advocacy is accessible to everyone. You don't need a formal job or title to start making a difference.

If you volunteer with a nonprofit, help fellow families, or do anything that makes life easier for someone else, you are an advocate. Even if you consider yourself to be "just a parent" working to solve problems for your children, that is advocacy, too. *Every effort you make matters.*

Sometimes advocacy is a **marathon**, requiring years of sustained effort to move a single piece of legislation. Sometimes it's a **sprint**, like rallying a community to solve a specific problem at a specific time. But often, it is a **relay**. We work as hard as we can, for as long as we can, and then we pass the baton to someone else to carry the mission forward. Recognizing which race you are running is the first step in protecting your peace.

Advocacy is fundamentally about addressing struggles
and refusing to let them go unnoticed.

Advocacy in Action

Advocacy often works more quietly than we expect, involving continuous efforts to highlight the unnoticed issues that affect our daily lives—like fixing potholes.

You may recognize this in your own circles, just as I do in mine.

- **The Community Guardians:** I have friends who are amateur meteorologists. They created a local social media page to provide our community with storm predictions. They share their passion and teach us about the science of weather so that we can keep our families safe. **This is advocacy.**

- **The Educational Navigators:** I have friends who work behind the scenes to ensure that children with special needs receive the specific services and accommodations they deserve within the school system. They bridge the gap between a child's potential and the school's resources. **This is advocacy.**

- **The Medical Translators:** I know parents who have mastered the insurance appeals process, spending hours on the phone to explain to corporate clerks why certain therapies are medical necessities rather than luxuries. They are rewriting the rules of access, one phone call at a time. **This is advocacy.**

- **The Neighborhood Fixers:** Friends of mine were dealing with an infestation of black vultures in their neighborhood that was causing damage to homes. They asked questions and eventually connected with the USDA, where they found someone who could help solve the problem. **This is advocacy.**

The Instinct and the Infrastructure

As a parent, I have often found myself in the role of advocate. My first odyssey began with Tori and her rare disease diagnosis, but my advocacy journey did not end there.

When our twins were three years old, I noticed they had a speech delay. I brought my concerns to our pediatrician, but she dismissed them for two consecutive years. In those moments, I faced a common dilemma that every advocate eventually encounters: Should I press the issue or remain polite?

Fearing that I might be labeled a "paranoid mom," I regrettably chose to stay quiet, choosing to be likable over being vocal. Imagine our shock when our boys came home from kindergarten with failed hearing screenings. They didn't just have a speech delay; they had *hearing loss*.

This revelation began a new phase of advocacy—one that I engage in daily. Fortunately, I wasn't starting from scratch. The skills I developed in the halls of the Capitol and in exam rooms with Tori provided the blueprint. I realized that while the pothole is different—hearing aids instead of oxygen tanks—the blueprint for fixing the system is essentially the same.

The Trap of the Label

We often remain silent because we fear being labeled "that person." We worry that our passion for our cause will be mistaken for paranoia, leading to our concerns being dismissed.

This is why we need the *Twelve Threads*.

When you have the **Yellow Thread** of data and the **Silver Thread** of neutrality, you don't have to worry about being perceived as a "paranoid mom." You become a technical partner. You aren't just a parent with an instinct; you are an architect with observations.

Many advocates fear that lacking credentials makes them imposters. In reality, *your lived experience is the ultimate credential.* A lobbyist may memorize a fact sheet, but only you can speak to the daily reality of the system's potholes. When you combine your raw passion with the *Twelve Threads*, you become a force that no degree can replicate. We all possess skills and experiences that can contribute to making the world a better, safer, and happier place. By embracing your role as an advocate, you can focus your energy on creating tangible impacts, leading to numerous positive outcomes for yourself and your community.

The Anatomy of Impact: Advocacy vs. Lobbying

One of the most significant barriers to action is the fear of doing it "wrong." We worry about credentials, titles, and legalities. However, in the *Brighter Blueprint*, we simplify the process. Essentially, advocacy is the environment and lobbying is an instrument. Every lobbyist is an advocate, but not every advocate is a lobbyist. While lobbying focuses on changing the rules (laws), advocacy aims to change the reality (awareness, access, and culture).

Note: *This manual provides strategic frameworks and is not intended as legal or tax advice regarding non-profit lobbying regulations.*

At its core, **advocacy** is any intentional action taken to create change for a cause you care about. The *Alliance for Justice* defines it as "any action that speaks in favor of, recommends, argues for a cause, supports or defends, or pleads on behalf of others."[1]

Advocacy encompasses a broad range of activities, including awareness, mobilization, and education to garner compassion and support.

Lobbying, on the other hand, is a specific and highly regulated branch of advocacy. If advocacy is like building a fire to create warmth (awareness), lobbying is focusing that heat through a magnifying glass to achieve a particular result: legislative change. Lobbying involves direct communication with a legislator to influence a specific law.

Feature	Advocacy (The Environment)	Lobbying (The Instrument)
The Intent	To solve a community problem.	To change legal code or secure funding.
The Audience	The general public and stakeholders.	Specific decision-makers (Legislators).
The Credentials	Lived experience and your story.	Data combined with a specific "Ask."
The Limits	Unrestricted. Go as loud and long as you want.	Highly regulated by state and federal law.
Example	Sharing a "Day in the Life" video of a diagnosis.	Asking a Senator to co-sponsor a specific bill.

If you are unsure if you are lobbying, ask:

- *Is it a government official?*

- *Is there a specific bill?*

- *Is there a directive (an ask)?*

If the answer to **all three** is yes, you are likely *lobbying*.
If any are no, you are practicing general *advocacy*.

Needles and Looms

At the *Brighter Blueprint Studio*, we recognize two primary methods of weaving. Neither is inherently better; they simply have different structural capabilities.

The Individual Needle (Personal Advocacy): You are sharp and precise, able to navigate through the fabric of the system wherever you find a gap. You don't need the approval of a board of directors to express your thoughts. You are the instrument that initiates the stitch. Without the individual advocate moving through the gaps, the loom has nothing to bind together.[2]

The Collective Loom (Nonprofit Advocacy): Depending on their size and funding support, these are large-scale structures that produce a significant volume of resources and awareness. However, they must adhere to legal regulations (such as 501(c)(3) status). They move slowly, but they provide the structure that holds the individual stitches together.

The Universal Thread

I refer to rare disease advocacy often because that is where my journey began, but these lessons were reinforced in the earthquake debris of Haiti, the markets of North Africa, and beyond. I discovered that whether you are testifying before a state Senate committee or providing roofing supplies to a village in need, the fundamental principles of human impact remain consistent.

These insights have helped me grow as a person. They've transformed my life from feeling chaotic to feeling like a cohesive tapestry.

Each tapestry we create will look different. The design will vary, and you may use certain colors more than I do, depending on your specific goals. However, all *Twelve Threads* woven together will make you unstoppable.

One person's goal might be to change a law, while another's mission could save a life.

Both are forms of advocacy.

Both require the same threads.

The Myth of the Perfect Advocate

During my time in Tunisia, I spoke with artisans who wove rugs. As I admired my purchase, a woman told me something that surprised me: They purposely leave a flaw in every rug. In their culture, they believe that nothing is perfect, and to pretend otherwise is a falsehood. Knowing that the flaw is there is comforting.

The intentional flaw isn't a sign of weakness; it's a sign of structural honesty. In advocacy, the "perfect" advocate—the one who never admits ignorance—is brittle. They break the moment the system pushes back. By embracing the flaw, we move from being a solo hero to being a partner who is willing to learn and recalibrate.

Few of us start as experts. If you are like me, this path chose you. I have observed time and time again that the most effective solutions come not from those with the most degrees, but from those who have felt the dust on their feet.

> Your most powerful tool is your own story. You don't have to be a policy expert; you just have to be an expert on your own life.
>
> Dr. Lisa Airan

Having *dust on your feet* means you have data that a PhD cannot access. You know where the potholes are because you've tripped in them. Your "flaw"—your lack of a formal degree—is actually your weaver's edge.

Whether it's rare disease, access to clean water, fair housing, or anything else, we must transition from the individual to the cause:
- The **individual** is the heartbeat, providing the *why*.
- The **cause** is the circulatory system, detailing the *how* for others.

By advocating for the cause, you protect people you may never meet.

None of us is perfect. We all learn as we go and make mistakes, which makes learning from one another invaluable. You do not need a formal education in political science or law to make a difference; all you need is the passion to address a problem.

As you pick up these *Twelve Threads*, remember the Tunisian rug. Do not wait for a perfect draft before you walk into the room. The system doesn't need a perfect orator; it needs an architect who is willing to dissect the problem, listen to the friction, and tie a knot that holds—flaws and all.

All advocacy is, at its core, an exercise in empathy.

Samantha Power

Language of the Loom
Weaving Terminology

In the *Brighter Blueprint*, we use the ancient art of weaving to describe the modern science of systemic change.

The Loom (The System)

The overarching framework—the laws, regulations, and bureaucracies—within which we work. The loom is not the enemy; it is the structure that allows the fabric to be made.

The Warp (The Anchor/Foundation)

The set of vertical threads held in high tension on the loom. In advocacy, the **warp** is your internal character: your resilience, humility, and neutrality. If these threads are weak or loose, the entire mission will collapse under pressure.

The Weft (The Weave/Influence)

The horizontal threads that are woven through the warp. It represents social influence: your alliances, your story, and your collective mandate. It provides the bulk, color, and visible impact of the mission.

The Shuttle (The Momentum/Action)

The tool used to carry the weft thread back and forth through the warp. In advocacy, the shuttle represents the rhythmic, daily labor of taking action and pivoting when obstacles arise.

The Draft (The Pattern/Intelligence)

The technical drawing or "blueprint" that the weaver follows. It represents the data, the diagnostic listening, and the strategic plan. You do not throw the shuttle until the **draft** is accurate.

The Tension (The Balance)

The pull on the threads. Too much tension and the thread snaps (**burnout**); too little tension and the fabric is saggy and weak (**ineffectiveness**). Mastery is the ability to maintain the perfect tension for the long haul.

The Snag (The Friction)

A knot or irregularity in the thread. **Snags** are internal or external obstacles—ego, partisan bias, or administrative "potholes"—that threaten to unravel the weave if not mended.

The Final Knot (The Permanence/Legacy)

The act of securing the edges of the fabric once it is removed from the loom. This represents **succession** and **automation**, ensuring the system continues to function permanently without the original weavers.

Setting the Anchor
Section One

Advocacy begins with self-reflection. Before you can influence a system, it's essential to address the tensions within your own foundation. Accepting that the back of the tapestry is often chaotic allows you to remain calm at the loom. You aren't losing control; you're simply witnessing the complexity required to create something beautiful. By setting **The Anchor**, you're doing more than just preparing; you're ensuring that when the system pushes back, your structure remains unshakeable.

The Three Pillars of the Weaver's Mindset:

- **Maintain Resilience (Pink Thread):** The endurance to stay in the loom for the long haul.

- **Practice Humility (White Thread):** The ability to partner with others, valuing learning over being the expert.

- **Bridge the Divide (Silver Thread):** A bridge-building identity that prioritizes the mission above political divisions.

Maintain Resilience
The Pink Thread

Background Music: I Still Haven't Found What I'm Looking For (U2)

Resilience is not a destination where you finally arrive and rest; it is the rhythmic and persistent movement of a soul that refuses to settle for a broken status quo. While we have "scaled city walls," we still wake up every morning and pick up the broom. Resilience is the strength to keep seeking the ideal while working within reality.

Key Idea: The pursuit of joy is a strategic choice to seek out restorative moments that replenish your emotional reserves and build resilience.

What helps you persevere is
your resilience and commitment.

Roy T. Bennett

Why Start With Resilience

You might find it unusual to begin a book about effective advocacy by discussing the need for resilience and burnout prevention, hinting at the potentially long and tiring journey ahead. However, honesty is essential. It's no secret that advocacy can be challenging work, especially when driven by pain. Burnout is a real risk, but I encourage you not to be discouraged. Resilience helps prevent burnout and forms the foundation for effective advocacy.

The **Pink Thread** symbolizes the often-overlooked yet vital act of discovering and choosing joy in your advocacy. This isn't about denying the pain that fuels your work; it's about developing emotional resilience to sustain your efforts. Without a plan for our own sustainability, we're not building a movement; we're simply waiting for our own collapse. In this context, joy isn't a luxury or a reward for a job well done—it's the fuel that keeps the other eleven threads functioning.

If you are a broken thread, the entire tapestry will eventually unravel.

Joy as a Tool, Not a Feeling

While each of us pursues different causes, these pursuits often stem from powerful emotions of pain, injustice, grief, or frustration. The energy they provide is limited, and if we rely solely on these feelings, we risk running on empty and eventually burning out. This discussion emphasizes the importance of actively seeking joy and rest to build resilience. The emotional energy that drives us cannot sustain us in the long term.

In this context, joy is not a trivial emotion. It represents the small, restorative moments that rejuvenate our spirits: sharing camaraderie with a fellow advocate, feeling accomplished after a productive meeting, or enjoying a quiet evening with family. **These moments are not distractions from our work; they sustain it.**

It may seem counterintuitive to focus on joy when your advocacy stems from trauma. You might feel guilty or think that experiencing joy diminishes the seriousness of your cause. This is a familiar and understandable feeling, but it can also be a trap. The world doesn't need another advocate who burns out after a year; it needs advocates who can persevere until the finish line.

Your burnout doesn't benefit your cause.

For me, joy doesn't replace the pain of losing my daughter; instead, they coexist daily, each vying for my attention. From experience, I know that without consciously seeking joy and rest, this journey can become overwhelming. If we don't commit to resilience and joy, and instead ignore the need for rest, the other essential aspects of advocacy become irrelevant.

A composer places a rest with intention,
knowing that silence is what makes the music sing.
It's time we started honoring the pauses in our own lives
with that same intentionality.

Mary Morlino

Applying the Pink Thread to Advocacy

The **Pink Thread** emphasizes the necessity of intentionally building time for joy and rest, especially during intense seasons. Recently, after a period of extensive travel and tight schedules, I felt burnt out and exhausted. When I unexpectedly had a few free hours, I chose to explore the city I was in. I walked for miles, observing the architectural details, tasting local cuisine, and enjoying my new surroundings. That evening taught me a valuable lesson: taking time for myself doesn't detract from my advocacy; it fuels my ability to contribute more effectively to the causes I support. Now, whenever I can, I set aside a couple of hours to wander, explore, and take pictures. This practice re-energizes me, especially during stressful events that require me to relive my challenging journey.

Your joy-sustaining practices may differ: it might be ordering dinner instead of cooking, taking a daily walk, or carving out time for a hobby. Effective advocacy requires deliberately incorporating joy into our work, ensuring that our emotional fuel never runs dry.

Resilience is the difference between a reactive campaign and a sustainable movement. If it's difficult to find joy in your cause, seek it elsewhere to sustain your resilience.

Resilience is not a trait you are born with; it is something you develop. In weaving, the strongest fabrics are created when the threads are subjected to consistent, calculated tension. If the threads are always loose, the tapestry lacks form. If they are pulled too hard without a break, they snap. Each time you stay engaged despite legislative setbacks, clinical challenges, or moments of deep grief, your resilience strengthens. **It is earned through the very obstacles that threaten to overwhelm you.** Your past trauma and current struggles are not merely obstacles; they serve as training for your mission. The goal of this process is not to avoid tension, but to master recovery.

You grow resilient not by avoiding the storm, but by continuing to prove to yourself that you can survive setbacks.

Recognizing the Signs of Burnout

Burnout is not a sign of weakness; rather, it is a predictable outcome of prolonged stress. Recognizing its signs in yourself and your fellow advocates is crucial for prevention. I speak from experience, as I am still learning to identify the early signs of burnout. Once burnout sets in, recovery can be quite challenging.

Here are three common indicators to watch for:

Emotional Exhaustion: A persistent feeling of being drained, overwhelmed, or fatigued, leaving you with nothing left to give.

Cynicism: A growing detachment from your work and a loss of faith in your ability to make a difference. The initial passion begins to fade.

Ineffectiveness: A sense of stagnation or a feeling that you are not accomplishing anything meaningful.

The Lifeline of Resilience

Advocacy work often begins in a deep place of grief, where pain is transformed into purpose. However, as you navigate the complex phases of policy change, it's easy to become overwhelmed by the process and lose sight of that initial motivation. The bureaucratic details—what to do, how to do it, and when—can overshadow the emotional aspects of who and why you started this journey.

To maintain your resilience, it's crucial to connect with your *why*. Burnout commonly occurs when the *what* (the emails, meetings, travel) becomes detached from the *who* and the *why* (the child, the patient, the future). Before you craft your strategy, you need to define the vision at the heart of your purpose.

Take a moment to reflect. What is your *why*? Is it the memory of a loved one, the hope for future generations, or the commitment to delivering a faster diagnosis? In the realm of advocacy, your *why* acts as your anchor. It's your source of strength. When a legislator tells you "no," a clinical trial fails, or any other obstacle arises, the *what* may be affected, but your *why* remains intact. This distinction allows you, as an advocate, to wake up the next day and continue your efforts.

If your identity is solely tied to victories, you will falter with every defeat. However, if your identity is rooted in your *why*, you'll remain resilient. Remembering your anchor will help you stay strong and choose rest strategically along your path.

A recommended resource for this idea is the book *Start With Why* by Simon Sinek,[1] as well as his related TED Talk.[2] He demonstrates in profound ways the importance of knowing why you do what you do.

The Presence of Purpose

In 2010, I traveled to Port-au-Prince, Haiti, to assist with earthquake relief. As we drove from the airport to our accommodations, I couldn't take my eyes off the devastation outside my window. The destruction was overwhelming—every street was filled with piles of gray concrete rubble. Where do you even begin when an entire city has been reduced to ruins?

Despite the chaos and destruction all around them, the resilient people of Haiti found a firmer foundation to live on—right in the median of the main road—until they could rebuild.

Living in the Median (Port-au-Prince, 2010)

While it wasn't ideal, with cars passing on either side of their makeshift homes, it provided some shelter from the sweltering heat of the day. They constructed what they hoped would be temporary dwellings using corrugated metal for walls, and their "yard" consisted of a two-foot space between a curb and a line of tires. This setup offered them a sense of peace and a reprieve from the fear that accompanied the ongoing aftershocks. It was easy to feel compassion for these brave souls.

One day, as we drove by the median, I noticed something and quickly grabbed my camera: a woman in a bright pink shirt was *sweeping*. Amid the exhaust fumes and gray dust from the collapsed buildings, she was cleaning her front porch. She was doing what she could with what she had to make her temporary home comfortable.

This is the essence of resilience at its purest.

Most people think of resilience as a feeling—a type of grit that some possess and others do not. However, in advocacy, resilience is a discipline. **It is the refusal to allow your environment to dictate your dignity.**

**Resilience isn't about the absence of rubble;
it's about the presence of purpose within it.**

The woman in the median didn't wait for the city to be rebuilt before she started sweeping. She didn't wait for a firm foundation to begin her work. She took the imperfect foundation she had and began to maintain it. Sweeping may have felt futile, but it gave her purpose—something to focus on while her world crumbled around her. She wasn't sweeping because the dust was gone; she was sweeping because her *why* (her dignity and sense of home) served as her anchor.

When we zoom in with curiosity, we find beauty and inspiration.

The Median in Your Advocacy

When fighting for a cause, whether it's a new law, a medical bill, or a local improvement, the rubble can often feel insurmountable. You may feel as if you are living in the median of a roaring street with traffic (opposition, bureaucracy, and exhaustion) rushing past you.

The **Pink Thread** asks you: **What is your broom?**

It's not about the scale: You may not be able to fix the whole city today, but you can clean your own front porch.

It's about the rhythm: The act of sweeping is a ritual that reminds you that you are still here and in charge of your own space.

It's about the change in YOU: We sweep the road knowing it will get dusty again and that the very act of sweeping is changing us. In advocacy, if you wait for the dust to settle before taking action, you will never make progress. You must learn to find your purpose while the traffic is still moving.

Practical Tools for Strategic Rest

In my years navigating public policy and advocacy, I have learned a crucial truth: **The most brilliant strategy is useless if the person carrying it out is too exhausted to execute it.**

When you rest, you are not only helping yourself; you are also signaling to those around you that the mission is stable enough to survive a pause. Strategic rest is an act of leadership that gives others permission to be human, too. It is connected to flexibility (**Purple Thread**)—a necessary pivot to ensure your well-being. Managing your emotional labor, setting boundaries, and leaning on your community are key components of strategic rest and help you maximize your impact without sacrificing yourself.

> Rest is a confession and a communication I make to those nearest me that I am aware of my limitations, that I am comfortable with them, and that they can be, too.
>
> Justin McRoberts

Acknowledge and Manage Emotional Labor

The grief, anger, or frustration that may motivate you can be powerful, but they are also heavy burdens. Acknowledge that you are on a long and challenging journey, and recognize that it's okay to feel overwhelmed. Your emotional well-being is a resource to manage, not an endless source of energy.

Most people operate with a low-resolution emotional display, meaning that they are unable to truly define how they feel. They feel bad, stressed, or upset. **Emotional Granularity**[3]—the psychological ability to name your feelings with high-definition precision—can help make your journey more sustainable.

Think of it as the difference between an old TV and a 4K monitor.

- **Low Granularity:** When your resolution is low, every difficult experience is a global blur of distress. Because you can't see the individual "pixels" of your pain, you react with broad, heavy-handed coping mechanisms—like total withdrawal or burnout.

- **High Granularity:** You see the specific shades. You realize you aren't just overwhelmed; you are actually *fatigued* by the travel, *disappointed* by a specific committee vote, and simultaneously *grateful* for a partner's text.

Neuroscience shows that the act of labeling a specific emotion (e.g., *"I feel marginalized by that comment"* rather than just *"I'm mad"*) actually reduces activity in the amygdala—the brain's alarm center.[4] By naming the knot, you begin to untie it.

You cannot manage what you cannot name. When you give your pain a precise name, you strip it of its power to be a ghost and turn it into a guest—one that you can eventually ask to leave.

Boundaries and Community

It is not just okay to say "no"—it is essential. This is an act of self-preservation that helps you avoid overextending yourself. Saying no to a request that exceeds your capacity allows you to say yes to the work that truly matters in the long term. Treat your rest time with the same seriousness as a meeting with a legislator.

Extend the same grace to your fellow advocates, allowing them to set boundaries and rest. Give each other permission to step back whenever needed, without questions asked. Later, we will discuss the importance of collaboration (**Green Thread**), which is about more than just reaching goals: it emphasizes mutual support. Connect with other advocates and agree to share joyful moments and celebrate each other's successes. Share both your struggles and your small victories—you don't have to bear the burden alone.

Simple Actions to Maintain Resilience

Create a small wins journal or jar: Every time you achieve a small success—whether it's a returned email, a kind word from a fellow parent, or a productive phone call—write it down. On days when you feel drained or defeated, revisit these notes to remind yourself of the progress you're making.

Schedule advocacy-free time: Intentionally block out a few hours on your calendar each week for activities not related to your cause—like reading, walking, or simply sitting in silence. Taking a break from advocacy is not quitting. Spending time with family, pursuing hobbies, or unplugging for a day will help you return to your work invigorated and with renewed purpose. Allow yourself—and others—the permission to rest.

Complete a small change: When national news or the slow pace of legislation feels overwhelming, intentionally focus on something small and achievable. Fix a "pothole" in your house, garden, or local neighborhood. Remind yourself that you still have the power to create change, even if those changes seem small.

Build your resilience toolkit: Create a mental or physical collection of items that bring you comfort or help you de-stress. This could include a playlist for long drives, a list of empowering quotes, or a simple stress ball. Use this toolkit whenever you start to feel overwhelmed.

Reconnect with your *Why*: On challenging days, pause to look at a photo that reminds you of why you are passionate about this cause, read a supportive message from a family you've helped, or revisit your original motivation. This simple act can instantly re-energize your sense of purpose.

Read stories of ordinary people who changed the world: When I feel overwhelmed or inadequate, stories like those in *The Small and The Mighty* by Sharon McMahon[5] and *One Woman Can Change the World* by Ronne Rock[6] remind me that progress is more important than perfection. Many individuals who made a meaningful impact, such as those who filled potholes, never had monuments built in their honor, yet their actions continue to resonate today.

Resilience is accepting your new reality,
   even if it's less good than the one you had before.
   You can fight it, you can do nothing but scream
   about what you've lost, or you can accept that
   and try to pull together something that's good.[7]

                     Elizabeth Edwards

Finding Beauty in the Mess

During my time in the streets of Port-au-Prince, I was amazed by the beauty that persisted amidst the rubble. Shops remained open on the street in front of the buildings that once operated there, even as piles of concrete surrounded them. Vibrant colors filled the scene—some natural, some intentionally added—through buildings, umbrellas, clothing, fruit, and flowers, creating a stark contrast to the devastation around me. Little did I know I would witness a similar contrast within the people themselves.

Business as Usual (Port-au-Prince, 2010)

As we worked in the communities, assisting with both big and small tasks, I did what I do best: I observed. Each day left me humbled; the people we encountered were content with what they had, doing everything they could to brighten their surroundings, something I struggled to achieve at the time. I saw them working together with joy, contentment, and inner peace, despite their fears about returning to their homes.

This peace was evident in the way they maintained their sense of community, including opening shops and markets amid the debris. And, in a beautiful woman who enjoyed dinner outside her home in the median, seemingly unfazed by the cars and trucks passing by.

Life for them was far from easy, but they consistently found joy through their resilience. They understood that the rubble would be part of their reality for a long time, and by accepting that, they were able to move forward.

While your situation or cause may not be as severe as the post-earthquake conditions in Haiti, the same principle applies. We may not be able to control our circumstances, but we can choose how we respond and actively cultivate joy and rest in our daily lives.

Advocates often worry that prioritizing their own rest or joy is selfish or betrays the urgency of their mission. In reality, your resilience is the fuel that drives the entire movement. You cannot pour from an empty cup, and you cannot lead a community toward health if you neglect your own well-being. Protecting your peace does not mean you are stepping away from your work; it ensures you have the strength to see it through.

That is why we begin with resilience.

Living Around the Rubble (Port-au-Prince, 2010)

The Narrative Lens: Inside Out

Illustrating complex psychological concepts through film can be very effective. In watching *Inside Out* (Pixar), it's important to view the **Pink Thread** as a fundamental structural requirement rather than merely an emotional comfort.

The Strategic Pivot: The film revolves around the mind of a young girl named Riley. For years, the character Joy has managed this system, believing that constant happiness is the only measure of success. When a significant life crisis occurs, Joy attempts to suppress Sadness, viewing emotional vulnerability as a leak in the system. However, the more Joy tries to repress the natural tension of grief and change, the more Riley's foundational "Islands of Personality" begin to crumble.

The Insight: Pay attention to the moment when Joy finally steps back and allows Sadness to take the lead. This represents the concept of Strategic Reserve. By accepting the reality of exhaustion and grief, Riley manages to prevent a complete system collapse. Joy's most humbling moment comes when she realizes that she isn't the only emotion essential to accomplishing the mission. Her breakthrough happens when she develops granularity. She realizes that a single memory can be both blue (sad) and yellow (joyful) at the exact same time. This is **Emotional Complexity.** Your pain doesn't have to vanish for your joy to be valid; they are simply two different fibers in the same stitch.

Resilience is not about forced positivity; it is about having the courage to be a whole person and the bravery to slow down.

The Pink Interlocks: Sustainable Resilience

These interlocks ensure your resilience is reinforced by strategy, preventing you from burning out before the road is paved. Sustainability ensures the thread doesn't fray before the legacy is secure.

Interlock	The Asset	The Stitch
Pink + White Practice Humility	Guilt-Free Boundaries	Protect your rest by using humility to drop the weight of the world.
Pink + Silver Bridge the Divide	Humanized Diplomacy	Stay kind in polarized rooms by focusing on human values, protecting your inner peace from political erosion.
Pink + Yellow Learn & Unlearn	Curious Endurance	Turn heavy policy research into a discovery process, replacing expert pressure with the light of curiosity.
Pink + Blue Listen for the Unspoken	Empathy Buffer	Hold space for community pain without absorbing it; listen to your own limits as closely as you listen to others.
Pink + Red Speak with Integrity	Joy of Justice	Find energy by ensuring the win reaches families, keeping the mission restorative rather than a list of tasks.
Pink + Gold Level the Loom	Community Care	Protect the collective energy of the alliance, valuing team resilience as a key performance indicator.
Pink + Green Forge Alliances	Sustainability Mandate	Treat your health as a moral obligation to the cause, aligning your personal integrity with your self-care.
Pink + Gray Lead Ethically	Resilient Rhetoric	Frame your pitch with hope rather than desperation, ensuring your message is fueled by wellness, not trauma.
Pink + Orange Share the Credit	Replenishing Joy	Refill your tank by celebrating the success of your peers, finding self-worth in collective progress not envy.
Pink + Brown Act Strategically	Paced Execution	Take action at a speed that prevents collapse, choosing long-term consistency over a sprint.
Pink + Purple Master the Pivot	Adaptive Peace	Maintain internal stability during a pivot, keeping a fluid mind to avoid the stress of rigid expectations.

Thread Experiment: The Joy Audit

The Task: Look at your calendar for the upcoming week. Highlight one non-work activity purely for your restoration. If nothing is scheduled, set aside a thirty-minute "Pink Block."

The Mastery: Resilience is not a reward for finishing your work; it is the fuel that allows the work to continue. An effective advocate knows that a burnt-out person is like a broken thread.

Bonus Experiments

Reflect on the past month of your life. What was your most joyful moment? What was your most draining moment?

Part of building resilience is knowing yourself and your strengths. If you haven't yet taken the *CliftonStrengths* assessment by Gallup, I highly recommend it!

Mirror Reflection

Am I treating myself with the same dignity and urgency that I demand for the people I serve?

Pink Thread Recap

You have prioritized your personal well-being and emotional inventory, acknowledging that a burned-out weaver cannot finish the tapestry.

The Result: You are grounded and replenished for the journey.

The Next Stitch: Now that you've secured your own internal peace, we move to the **White Thread**, where we learn the quiet strength of **humility**—recognizing that while your experience is unique, you are part of a much larger story.

Don't ask what the world needs. Ask what makes you come alive and go do it. Because what the world needs is people who have come alive.

Attributed to Howard Thurman

Practice Humility
The White Thread

Background Music: Beautiful Day (U2)

Your passion cannot replace expertise. This song symbolizes the moment you step outside your own ego and recognize that you are a student in a much larger world. Humility is the "Beautiful Day" when you stop trying to control everything and begin to learn from everyone. It changes your perspective from "They are blocking me" to "We are all part of this system together."

Key Idea: Humility allows you to acknowledge your own limitations and appreciate others' expertise, ensuring that your advocacy is grounded in collaboration rather than arrogance.

Humility is not thinking less of yourself,
it's thinking of yourself less.

Attributed to C.S. Lewis

From Resilience to Humility

In the previous chapter, we explored the importance of resilience, noting that personal resilience and joy are essential for sustainability. However, grounding yourself in self-care is only the first step. To effectively engage with a vast and complex system in order to change it, you must replace personal certainty with *humility*—the quiet strength that enables you to see yourself as a dedicated partner rather than a solitary warrior.

The Warp and the Weft: The Architecture of Humility

In weaving, the warp consists of the threads that run lengthwise on the loom. These threads are held taut and parallel, forming the fabric's foundational structure. The weft, on the other hand, refers to the threads that are woven crosswise, over and under the warp.

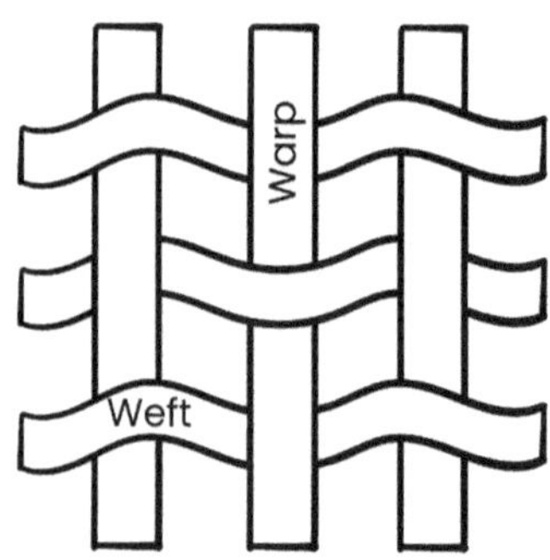

Humility serves as the warp of your advocacy. It provides an unwavering foundation that prevents your efforts from unraveling. Humility is the tension that allows the other threads of advocacy to be woven together, enabling the fabric of your work to flex under pressure without breaking. Humility does not mean belittling your efforts or shrinking your cause; instead, it represents quiet strength. By recognizing that you are part of a much larger, ongoing story, you can stay persistent and confident while remaining open to the world around you.

Admittedly, I am embarrassed when I reflect back on my initial months of advocacy. My anger and grief fueled an overconfidence in my knowledge, which led to mistakes. I had no idea what I was doing, and it took me far too long to realize my personal limitations. I initially believed my role was to *demand change*, when in fact it was to *ask for help*. I quickly learned that my lived experience, while powerful, was not the only form of expertise that mattered.

Embracing humility became a life-changing lesson, bringing me freedom and peace as an advocate and as a person.

The Road Taken (or Not Taken)

The ultimate goal of your advocacy journey—whether it leads to a new policy or increased awareness—is undeniably important. However, the *path* you take to achieve that goal, including ethical considerations, collaboration, and respect for all stakeholders, defines the integrity and lasting impact of your advocacy.

> Two roads diverged in a wood, and I—I took the one less traveled by, and that has made all the difference.
>
> Robert Frost

As the famous poem by Robert Frost illustrates, we have a choice: we can take the road most traveled, pushing our way to victory without considering the unintended consequences, or we can choose the road less traveled—one marked by humility, collaboration, and an awareness of the broader systemic impact of our actions. Advocacy should focus on building a better system, not merely winning a battle, and this philosophy guides our entire framework.

Simply put, humility is the ability and willingness to acknowledge what you don't know and to recognize that everyone—from public health officials and legislators to fellow parents—has valuable knowledge and perspectives to contribute.

This humility signifies inner strength and prevents the kind of arrogance that can alienate allies and stifle growth opportunities. It is indeed the road less traveled, making every step worthwhile.

Advocacy is a mission, not a monument to the advocate.

Own Your Mistakes

Humility isn't a soft virtue; it's a critical data-gathering strategy. If you are too proud to admit what you don't know, you risk making strategic errors later on. Humility is the tool that ensures your message remains accurate.

In advocacy, you will inevitably make a mistake. You might misquote a statistic, miss a deadline, or misread a stakeholder's intent. In those moments, your ego may urge you to double down, deflect blame, or use creative language to save face. **Resist that urge. Own the error.** Your passion is not a shield against your mistakes.

When you make a mistake, acknowledge it immediately and clearly. Do not blame the system, gaslight your partners, or lie to stakeholders. Prioritize the objective truth over your personal comfort. This is where humility meets learning and unlearning (**Yellow Thread**). You admit you aren't the sole source of truth, and you prioritize the verified data point over your personal pride. By acknowledging the error, you actually enhance your credibility. Stakeholders will trust you more because they know you aren't afraid of the truth—even when it contradicts your talking points.

Humility is the ability to say, "I was wrong, and here's how I will fix it," without feeling erased.

The Effective Advocate's Recovery Script

Acknowledge: "I realized that the data I provided yesterday regarding [topic] was incorrect/incomplete."

Correct: "The accurate figure is [X], verified by [source]."

Bridge: "I apologize for the oversight. I've updated my brief to ensure we are working from the most accurate foundation moving forward."

Accuracy Over Ego

In advocacy, pride is the silent killer of progress. It makes us double down when we are wrong because we've tied our identity to a specific position. But I have learned a freeing truth:

I would rather be accurate than right.

Admitting you were misled isn't a sign of weakness; it's a sign of integrity. Humility is the willingness to say, "I don't know, but let me learn from the experts." It is the strength required to normalize changing your mind when presented with new facts.

In the heat of a meeting or a public hearing, you might be corrected by a stakeholder, researcher, or even an opponent. Your natural "fight or flight" response may tempt you to argue, minimize the error, or change the subject.

The White Thread move is to pause and pivot to gratitude.

Stop seeing a correction as an attack on your authority and start seeing it as a **gift of accuracy.** Every time someone corrects a fact for you, they are preventing you from building a skyscraper on a foundation of sand. Thank them. Genuinely. By saying, *"Thank you for correcting that; it's vital that we are working from the most accurate data possible,"* you immediately disarm the "gotcha" moment. You prove that you are a technical partner who values the integrity of the solution more than the win of the argument.

I've learned that when I feel offended by something, or when I learn new information that goes against what I believe, I've been given the perfect opportunity to sit in that feeling for a while—not brush it off and assume I'm right—and to take the time to learn more about the other side of whatever that something may be. I may not end up changing my position, but I will have more compassion and understanding for those who see things that way.

The Unfused Identity: Holding Ideas Loosely

One of the most significant dangers in advocacy is the psychological concept of *Identity Fusion*.[1] This occurs when we stop merely holding a belief and start embodying it. For example, if you identify as "The Person Who Is Right About This," then any evidence that contradicts your stance feels like an attack on your very existence.

Your ideas are tools, not your identity.

When you hold your ideas loosely, you become a more effective advocate because you are no longer blinded by the need to defend your ego. Instead, you focus on pursuing accuracy rather than seeking vindication. This is the structural secret of the **White Thread.** When your identity is rooted in being an effective advocate, your ideas are merely tools—and you're always willing to replace a dull tool with a sharper one.

Another helpful approach is to treat everything as a draft that can be edited, reviewed, and enhanced. Drafts are meant to change, and the creator should not feel insulted when revisions are made that strengthen the effort. When you separate your self-worth from your current strategy, you can pivot more quickly, you hear the stakeholder feedback because you weren't preparing your defense, and your resilience (**Pink Thread**) remains intact because your worth is not dependent on others agreeing with you.

If you can't walk away from your favorite idea when a better one arrives, you aren't a weaver; you're a prisoner of your own pride.

Applying the White Thread to Advocacy

I have noticed two common scenarios in advocacy: approaching it with arrogance or feeling like an imposter or outsider. Many advocates experience imposter syndrome, feeling unqualified compared to doctors or policymakers. Even while writing this book, I have often struggled with imposter syndrome, wondering if this work is meaningful and worth the reader's time, wondering *who am I to write this?* In moments when you feel out of place or like an imposter, remember that your personal story is a unique form of expertise that no one else possesses—and **you wouldn't want anyone else to have it,** as it's what drives your advocacy. The entire reason for my advocacy work is so other families don't suffer as we did. That alone makes me a valid participant.

Humility reminds us that while we may not know everything, what we do know can help others. You are a partner with a unique and invaluable perspective. As people who are directly impacted by our cause, we belong at the table. There is always room for more people, and addressing our challenges may require additional voices.

This quote sums it up perfectly:

If they don't give you a seat at the table,
bring a folding chair.

Shirley Chisholm

Bring the folding chair, but once you sit down, use it to listen as much as you use it to speak. Humility ensures that once you have your seat, you don't use it to build a wall.

A strategic advocate understands that:

- They don't need to be the smartest person in the room.

- It is more impactful to ask, **"What can I do to help you?"** than to say, **"You must do this."**

- Their inexperience can be an asset—fresh eyes that can see the potholes those already in the system may overlook.

No one expects you to have all the answers. It's perfectly fine to say, "That's a great question. I will learn more and let you know what I find." Don't discount your inexperience; your fresh perspective may help you identify issues that need attention more quickly than those accustomed to the status quo.

Humility is the crucial mindset that enables you, as an advocate, to listen and learn. You are the expert on your loved one and your family's experience, which drives your advocacy. However, you are not the expert on public health, state budgets, or legislative procedures. And that's okay.

Note: It's important to distinguish between feeling proud of your achievements and being too proud to seek help. I am proud of what I achieved in Tori's honor, but what I value most are the personal changes I experienced along the way, especially my growth in humility. I have become a better person through the lessons I've learned, and I now share them with you.

Advocates often fear that being humble means being quiet or passive. However, the opposite is true: humility is an active pursuit of truth and partnership. By lowering our egos, we actually enhance our impact in all areas.

When engaging with any government system, remember that you will meet people who have often dedicated their entire careers to public service. Humility allows us to respect their expertise and approach them with curiosity rather than confrontation, even if they don't return your curiosity. Ask questions first rather than leading with demands. Trust the process, even when it feels slow, because it is designed to be evidence-based and deliberate, minimizing unintended consequences. Acknowledge their work and the immense amount of unseen labor that goes into every aspect.

Embracing humility enables you to build the relationships necessary to achieve tasks that would otherwise remain unfinished and to open doors that might otherwise stay closed.

Recognizing Your Resources

When I arrived in Haiti, I was prepared to work hard and to face discomfort, both physical and emotional. Whenever I travel to a developing country, I am reminded of the immense privilege and relative wealth I possess, and I am fully aware that I will return home changed.

I entered Haiti without a job, living with relatives, and facing an uncertain future. However, I quickly recognized that I had a wealth of options, the luxury of a "home base" that wasn't just a concrete median, and the ability to leave a disaster zone when my week was over.

This realization marked my true initiation into the **White Thread**. True humility in advocacy means understanding that you are a **steward**, not a **savior**.

The Exit Strategy of the Ego

While at the Ft. Lauderdale airport on my way to Haiti, I overheard a Haitian man discussing the international community, stating, "They never finish the job." He was referring to "tourist advocates"—individuals who show up during moments of crisis but disappear once the tedious work of reconstruction begins. Initially, I was offended. He sounded so ungrateful and it would have been easy to dismiss his comments by framing them that way.

But he was right.

Humility is the choice to remain engaged in the challenging aftermath long after the initial excitement fades. In advocacy, this means persisting in the fight even when progress stalls, news cameras have moved on, and your own energy is waning.

Resources are tools, not trophies. Whether it's your platform, your budget for roofing supplies, or your political connections, these resources don't belong to you. They are the threads you've been given to weave into someone's life.

You must have the humility to acknowledge that your experience of a situation, such as encountering a pothole, differs from that of those who live in it every day. While I could leave the median, the woman sweeping her porch could not. My role wasn't to pity her, but to use my resources to help her rebuild.

The **White Thread** encourages you to reassess your "wealth"—your education, voice, and platform—without viewing them as personal achievements. Instead, see them as materials you have been sent to deliver. Once you witness the rubble, you cannot return to your previous perception of the world. The only humble response is to take up a tool and remain until the job is done.

The Narrative Lens: The Karate Kid

A movie that perfectly illustrates the **White Thread** is the original *The Karate Kid.* If you're not familiar with it, I encourage you to watch or rewatch it. The goal is to observe humility as a requirement for learning a new system.

The Strategic Pivot: Daniel enters the story wanting to learn to fight in order to confront a specific threat. He seeks guidance from Mr. Miyagi, the "expert," but becomes frustrated when Miyagi doesn't teach him any fighting moves. Instead, Miyagi assigns him menial tasks such as painting fences and waxing cars. Daniel's pivot occurs when he stops complaining about his unmet expectations from the expert and submits to the process. His anger initially makes him resist the "wax on, wax off" work. A lack of resilience (**Pink Thread**) leads to a lack of humility (**White Thread**).

The Insight: Watch for the famous "wax on, wax off" reveal. Daniel realizes that by being humble enough to engage in the dry, repetitive tasks without ego, he has been building the muscle memory and technical foundation necessary for mastery. In advocacy, this could look like researching budget items, and attending dull subcommittee hearings. Although it may feel like busywork, it actually constitutes the muscle memory needed for systemic success.

In advocacy, we often want to jump straight into the "fight" (the policy change). This movie demonstrates that you must first be humble enough to "paint the fence"—understanding the boring, administrative parts of the system, as well as learning about yourself—before you can hope to win the tournament.

The White Interlocks: Cultivate Humility

These interlocks anchor your mission in a service-first mindset. Lowering your ego to raise your impact isn't a sign of weakness; it's a strategic choice to ensure the focus is on the mission, not the person.

Interlock	The Asset	The Stitch
White + Pink Maintain Resilience	Quiet Strength	Accept help; prioritize collective resilience over recognition.
White + Silver Bridge the Divide	Neutral Convener	Ensure the cause is the story's hero; maintain neutrality by separating party from identity.
White + Yellow Learn & Unlearn	Clean Slate	Admit ignorance to find superior systemic solutions; drive learning through curiosity.
White + Blue Listen for the Unspoken	Deep Receptivity	Listen to understand, not to prepare a rebuttal; prioritize the system's needs over your own.
White + Red Speak with Integrity	Authentic Voice	Ensure your message lacks the ego that triggers skepticism; words reflect reality, not power.
White + Gold Level the Loom	Self-Aware Equity	Advocate for justice while checking your own bias; equity as is a partnership, not a rescue.
White + Green Forge Alliances	Relational Safety	Attract elite partners by avoiding turf wars; value collective success over credit.
White + Gray Lead Ethically	Teachable Integrity	Hold principles with a steady hand, but plans with a loose one; separate core values from pride.
White + Orange Share the Credit	Selfless Leadership	Fuel movement momentum by letting others shine; find pride in the mission's visibility.
White + Brown Act Strategically	Service-First Action	Fix potholes without requiring public accolades; focus on tangible results over validation.
White + Purple Master the Pivot	Fluid Humility	Pivot instantly because you aren't married to your plan; detach your identity from your strategy.

Thread Experiments: The Expert Swap

The Task: Identify someone in your network who possesses a skill you lack (this could be anything, from accounting to graphic design to deep-sea fishing). Ask them one genuine question: "How does that work?" or "What do you enjoy most about this?"

The Mastery: Advocacy isn't about being the smartest person in the room; it's about being the most curious. When you acknowledge your limits, you invite others to help fill those gaps.

Bonus Experiment

Spend five minutes researching a key stakeholder, ideally someone you disagree with. Find something in their history—such as an article, speech, or bill they supported—that you can sincerely acknowledge and commend. Then, take a minute to send them a message expressing your appreciation. This act of gratitude reflects humility and respect.

Mirror Reflections

Am I willing to normalize admitting when I'm wrong?

Am I defending this belief because it's the right one, or simply because it's mine? How many of my beliefs are merely assumptions I haven't tested?

White Thread Recap

You have checked your ego at the door, choosing the precision of accuracy over the satisfaction of being "right."

The Result: You have established a foundation of credibility that invites experts and stakeholders to trust your lead.

The Next Stitch: Now that you have anchored your mission in humility, we move to the **Silver Thread**, where we learn to build bridges across partisan divides, ensuring your cause is never benched by a political label.

Arrogance creates a mental block that prevents you
from taking in new information. Humility is
being open to the possibility that you might be wrong.[2]

Ray Dalio

Bridge the Divide
The Silver Thread

Background Music: On The Turning Away (Pink Floyd)

Nonpartisanship is often misunderstood as silence or a lack of conviction. In reality, it is a courageous and uplifting refusal to allow partisan indifference to divert you from your mission. It is a shield for those who walk the middle aisle, keeping the focus on alleviating suffering rather than winning an argument.

Key Idea: Nonpartisanship isn't neutrality; it is the conscious choice to prioritize your mission above all political affiliations. Your primary loyalty is to the truth and the well-being of people—not a party.

Compassion becomes real when we recognize
our shared humanity.[1]

Brené Brown

An Oasis in the Sahara

In 2005, I traveled to Tunisia for a month to live and learn with a group from my university. As an American woman, I encountered a culture with gender norms and religious practices that were very different from my own. I felt the friction of *different.* To be honest, there were moments when I felt physically and emotionally uncomfortable. We were required to dress very modestly despite the heat, I had to remain at home in the evenings with the other women while the men went out, and we couldn't look men in the eye, lest they assume ill intent.

View from our Window (Tunis, 2005)

Not all of the differences felt as serious; on the lighter side, there were only a handful of cereal options at the corner store compared to our American abundance, and we even ate tuna on pizza (yes, really). One of the first Arabic phrases we learned was "blech harissa," so we could refuse the spicy condiment that they loved to add to their food because it was far beyond our tolerance.

So much was different, but I discovered that *different* is not synonymous with bad or a matter of right versus wrong; it is simply different. While their way of life might have seemed simpler than mine in some respects, they were more advanced in others—many individuals were effortlessly bilingual or even trilingual. They were clever, creative, and resourceful. By humbly setting aside my assumptions, I had a life-changing experience. We didn't try to impose our way of living on them; instead, we entered their world and sought out our commonalities. We humanized them. It didn't matter that we held different beliefs or viewed the world through different lenses. By finding that common ground of mutual respect, we were able to build a bridge that allowed us to coexist and, more importantly, to learn from one another.

Bob Marley and White Sand

One of my favorite memories is from our time in the Sahara Desert. Our local guides were incredibly kind and funny; striving to overcome the language barrier, they played Bob Marley (in English) and Shakira (in Spanish)—music they thought we might enjoy. It certainly made the entire experience memorable, even though it wasn't the music we would have chosen. We recognized that they were building a bridge for us.

After we departed the oasis where we had spent the night, the color of the desert sand changed from orange to white. Our guide, Hedi, remembered that I had collected some orange sand earlier. He stopped the vehicle and, with his limited English and my extremely limited Arabic, he handed me a bag and excitedly gestured for me to collect some white sand as well.

I still have that sand today.

Though we were different in almost every way, we found common ground—and we even danced together to Bob Marley in the Sahara.

The Desert and the Oasis

In advocacy, we often find ourselves in the middle of a desert. It may feel desolate, hopeless, and lonely. We have a choice to make: we can wander in the heat of our own convictions, or search for the **oasis**—the place of bridge-building.

The oasis is not where you abandon your identity; it is where you trade judgment for curiosity. People come to the refuge of the oasis because they have common needs. You must respect the person across the table more than you dislike their system or stance.

When you enter a legislative office or a community meeting, you step into a subculture with its own rules and priorities. If I had spent my time in Tunisia judging people for their differences, I would have missed the beauty of who they were and the rhythm of our shared dance. Similarly, in your advocacy, if you focus solely on judging your "opponents," you risk missing opportunities to find allies who may be hidden behind a different perspective or political affiliation.

To be an effective advocate, you must speak the language of the room you are in. When you lead with respect for the individual, you earn the right to discuss policy. You don't have to agree with everything someone believes to work with them on a piece of legislation or to solve a shared problem. You don't have to share a worldview to acknowledge a shared pothole. And the more compassion you have for yourself, the greater your resilience and your ability to work with those who see things differently than you do.[2]

In the desert of division, the master weaver doesn't wait for a storm to change the landscape; they build an oasis through respect.

The Paradox of Trust

There are two things I hope you take away from this chapter:

First, we are more similar than we want to believe.

Second, we are being manipulated into thinking we aren't.

In the world of sports, team loyalty really matters to some. While some fans seem to care only when the team is winning, others are loyal to their team(s) no matter what. It becomes part of their identity, and their dislike for the other team (and its fans) can run deep.

Yet, when the athletes from our chosen teams take off their jerseys, they are simply humans. If you don't know what they look like, you can't tell the difference between teams. The rivalry is more difficult to maintain if you don't know which team someone plays for.

Seth Godin notes that we are living in a "moment in time when more people are connected and fewer are trusted. When science and fact are often thrown into a blender of willful misinterpretation and hurried misunderstanding."[3]

We certainly see this in the United States, where many have been conditioned to show profound distrust toward experts (scientists, economists)[4] while showing unquestioning loyalty to political figures. Why?

Because partisanship has become a mental shortcut.

It tells us that we don't need to learn (**Yellow Thread**) or listen (**Blue Thread**); just check the jersey. It makes us believe there are separate sets of facts, and we can disregard any facts from the other side without verifying them. We have been told repeatedly that our team is the only one to be trusted, and eventually, we believe it. Loyalty to the party becomes part of who we are.[5]

When we allow partisanship to dictate our thinking, we become vulnerable. And not only us as individuals, but also collectively as a country and even the world. As Jonathan Haidt notes in his book, *The Righteous Mind*, "America's hyperpartisanship is now a threat to the world."[6]

If the price of political loyalty is the dismissal of verifiable truth, the system fails the very people it was designed to protect.

The Algorithm of Fear

Even more frustrating to me is the fact that this partisan division isn't accidental; it's engineered. As marketing professional Kirk Grogan observes, we have reached a moment when data isn't just used to understand us—it's used to proactively **shape our beliefs**.[7] In advocacy and in daily life, the "Dark Side" of data isn't just about selling you a product; it's about selling you a specific version of your neighbor as an enemy.

Algorithms are designed to funnel you toward a goal by instilling a fear of being controlled and dividing us. They create echo chambers that reinforce your existing biases. By targeting both sides of an issue with fear-based narratives, the system ensures the weave of society remains too frayed to function.

Here are a few ways this polarization is manufactured:

The Polarization Trap

We often think that exposure is the cure for division. However, research by Bail et al. (2018)[8] shows a backfire effect: exposing people to opposing views on social media can actually *increase* their political polarization.[9] Without neutrality (**Silver Thread**), the brain treats different perspectives as a threat to be defeated.

The Architecture of the Echo

As Cinelli et al. (2021)[10] documented, social media platforms are structurally biased toward ideological homogeneity. The internet is built to amplify your existing ideas.

The Cost of the Bridge

Garimella et al. (2018)[11] found that users who attempt to bridge echo chambers often lose social status within their own circles. This is why humility (**White Thread**) is a requirement. You must be willing to lose status in the echo chamber to gain impact in the system.

The Misinformation Weave

Del Vicario et al. (2016)[12] observed that misinformation and truth spread through the same structural patterns. The only thing that stops a frayed end from becoming a flawed fabric is rigorous data integrity (**Yellow Thread**).

Truth is a pin. One well-placed, accurate fact can burst a thousand-person echo chamber. Do not let the algorithm write your narrative; be the author of your own data.

Finding Common Ground

Enjoying different sports teams doesn't have to make us enemies. And neither does seeing things differently. We can choose to adjust our vision to learn more about what the other sees. Living our lives differently doesn't have to create a wall between us; we can choose to build a bridge and focus on the similarities. The difference is in our willingness to learn, to listen to understand, and to be open to changing our minds; in truly loving our neighbors, not hating them because they live differently than we'd choose to live, and not imposing our belief system on their lives. The difference is in humbly recognizing that we could be wrong.

Diversity, coupled with humility, makes us stronger.

The idea of *connectivity*, defined as "*a willingness to prioritize relationships over competitiveness and engage in conversation with one's political adversaries to genuinely understand their viewpoints*"[13] is critical in advocacy. Without the trust that *connectivity* brings, ideas will remain partisan and the willingness to deliberate will be low.

Many challenges, especially in areas like public health, transcend political party lines. Therefore, solutions to these problems must be rooted in unity rather than division. To succeed, you must set aside political beliefs to find common ground, because the cause for which you are fighting is likely a human issue, not a partisan one.

Pennsylvania Capitol at Sunset

When Partisanship Stands in the Way

In 2019, I witnessed firsthand the damaging effects of party loyalty. During my second attempt to reform the state's Newborn Screening system, my bill was mysteriously stalled. Seeking answers, I approached the Speaker of the House's policy advisor. As he reviewed the bill and its history, he delivered fourteen words that shattered my perspective:

"Your bill is dead. They don't want to give a Philly [party] a win."

Nothing had prepared me for those words and I was speechless. I scrambled to come up with a response, but all I could say was, "What now?" Babies with rare, treatable conditions were being ignored simply because of the party affiliation of one of the sponsors.

Rarely are decisions immediately obvious to me, but this moment changed everything: *I became nonpartisan.* There are so many problems to be solved, and so much time is wasted because of partisanship. That day began an unraveling of my identity and the beginning of taking the road less traveled.

Solving problems is a mission; sabotaging solutions because of a party label is a *choice*—one I refuse to make.

The Silent Enemy

In the years since, I have come to realize that *Identity Fusion*—the psychological tendency to tie our self-worth to a label[14]—is a silent enemy of advocacy. When our main identity is partisan, critiquing party leaders feels like an attack on ourselves. This defensiveness hinders our ability to objectively analyze a policy's flaws, even when the data indicates the approach is ineffective or wrong.

I firmly believe that your identity should not be tied to the party you support. *You are more than your opinions.*

I know this is an unpopular opinion, but no political party deserves unwavering loyalty. No leader or organization is perfect, and many do not have our collective best interest in mind. Your true allegiance should be to your principles, not a label.

> As we take sides, lose trust, and get angrier and angrier, we not only solidify an idea of our enemy, but also start to lose our ability to listen, communicate, and practice even a modicum of empathy.[15]
>
> Brené Brown

Theologian Scot McKnight notes[16] that many people protect their story and identity so vociferously that they denounce even solid, unassailable facts as fraudulent. They realize there is too much to lose if their story—their identity—changes. Honest people strive for a **transparent story** that invites correction.

The **Silver Thread** (and a functioning democracy) requires that you maintain the moral clarity necessary to hold *everyone* accountable. You must call out harmful or unjust behavior and policies, even when it comes from your preferred side—*especially* in those cases. Independence empowers you to do this.

The divide in our country has grown so extreme that some leaders refuse to acknowledge good ideas from the opposition—as I experienced in 2019—while others blindly defend flawed ideas from their own party to stay in power. **I want no part of that broken dynamic.** Choosing principle over party ensures that the right thing is done, regardless of who originated the idea.

The Freedom of the Nonpartisan Advocate

Before that day in Harrisburg, I didn't realize how much of my identity was shaped by fear. Partisanship is designed to keep us in submission by not only telling us what to think, but also who—and what—to fear. When I chose principle over party, that fear evaporated. I stopped seeing legislators as enemies to be defeated and started viewing them as people to be persuaded. I understood that the laughing reactions on social media and the criticism from those in my life who didn't comprehend my shift were a small price to pay for the clarity of a clean conscience.

When you aren't on a "team," you are not required to defend the indefensible simply because your team proposed it. We are free to examine the fruit of the policy or behavior: *Is the policy/behavior encouraging peace, equity, and justice? Or is it encouraging outrage, dehumanization, and division? What about those in leadership?*

When we allow partisanship to become a mental shortcut, we stop looking at the fruit and start looking at the jersey. We justify actions and policies that contradict our deepest values simply because they were proposed by "our team." The **Silver Thread** isn't about being middle-of-the-road; it's about having a standard of conduct that applies to everyone equally. If you wouldn't accept a behavior from your enemy, you must not excuse it in your ally.

The Asymmetry of Error

In the heat of a political or legislative battle, we often become fused to our positions. We aren't just arguing for a policy; we are arguing for our own rightness. It is easy to see when an opponent is wrong, and much less obvious in ourselves. An effective advocate doesn't care about being right; they care about the structural integrity of the weave.

To evaluate a leader, a policy, or a path, we must ask ourselves this question: **"If we are wrong, what happens next?"**

By framing it this way, you aren't attacking someone's leader or team. You are inviting them to weigh the risk: it forces both parties to admit they could be wrong (**White Thread**); it prioritizes the vulnerable by asking, "Who pays the price for our mistake?" (**Gold Thread**).

Most importantly, it builds a bridge by allowing you to say, *"I hope you are right. If you are, we all win. But because I see a structural risk that you don't, I have to design a blueprint that accounts for the possibility that you might be wrong. Can we agree that a safety net is better than a free fall?"*

The **Silver Thread** isn't about having no opinion; it's about having a **standard of conduct** that applies to everyone equally. It is about standing firmly on the mission's high ground and inviting everyone else to join you there. You do not have to become personally nonpartisan to be an effective advocate; however, you must approach every conversation with a mindset of building bridges.

Throw out your assumptions. Be curious. Be respectful. It is the only way to weave a tapestry that actually covers everyone.

**Strategic neutrality is the bridge that carries
a mission across partisan divides.**

Applying the Silver Thread to Advocacy

This thread emphasizes making your work a unifying influence rather than a divisive one. By highlighting the common goal of assisting all individuals and families affected by the issue you're addressing, you can foster broad coalitions and gain bipartisan support for significant, lasting improvements.

Your commitment to nonpartisanship helps maintain a pure purpose in an environment designed for division. Partisan advocacy is not only ineffective but can also be actively destructive. It forces you to prioritize a political label over scientific data, human outcomes, and opportunities for collaboration across party lines. By engaging with people on common ground and striving for a shared goal—such as saving lives—you can rise above politics and build strong alliances.

A person's party membership can often serve as a mental shortcut, leading us to perceive them as obstacles to progress. In advocacy, it is essential to reject these labels and view individuals as unique. An approach focused on conflict and defeating an opponent often deepens divisions rather than alleviating them. Conversely, fostering unity creates a foundation for lasting progress, capable of enduring shifts in political leadership and ensuring that your efforts make a durable impact. When you adopt a nonpartisan stance in your advocacy, you can approach any office and present a solution based solely on its merits and data. A partisan stance limits you by immediately excluding half of the system.

We choose to:

- **Work with anyone:** We are free to engage the right lawmaker or stakeholder for the job—regardless of the letter next to their name. Individuals from a different party are not adversaries.

- **Prioritize the goal:** Our focus shifts entirely to the outcome rather than to taking credit. We approach every conversation with the intent to find common ground.

- **Maintain credibility:** When we publicly align ourselves with the best ideas from both sides, we demonstrate that our commitment is to the issue, not to political power.

> Partisanship is a choice,
> which means that using it as an excuse
> to leave problems unsolved is also a choice.

I understand from personal experience how challenging it can be to shift away from this mindset. By following these principles, I hope you can prioritize values over party allegiance in both advocacy and life, enabling us to tackle the issues we collectively face.

Nonpartisanship allows you to appeal to the conscience of any leader because you are humble (**White Thread**) enough to acknowledge that your perspective is limited and your ideas may be fallible. You aim to inspire stakeholders to set aside their partisan perspectives and embrace compassion. This transformation is possible only when your message remains genuine and nonpartisan.

View the "other side" not as enemies but as potential sources of data you may not have considered yet. You are not trying to win a fight; you are trying to solve a puzzle. If someone else has the missing piece, their side should not matter to you—you simply want to find the piece.

The Reinforcing Spiral

The **Spiral of Silence Theory**[17] suggests that if you believe your opinion is in the minority, you stay silent for fear of isolation. But in the digital age, the spiral has flipped. Instead of silence, we see echo chambers and polarization,[18] largely fed by social media platforms.[19] Algorithms serve to cement our opinions rather than challenge them. We find ourselves in bubbles where the minority feels emboldened to yell, and the majority often grows weary and retreats.

The Self-Silencing Trap

You may find yourself "spiraling into silence" not because you are wrong, but because the environment has become uncivil. There is a cost to this:

Personal: When we stop talking to those we disagree with, we lose our faith in democracy and our empathy for others.

Systemic: Without cross-cutting conversations, we can not solve problems. We stop being weavers and start being warriors, protecting our own bubble while the rest of the fabric frays.

How do we stop the spiral? How do we communicate when the system is designed to make us hate each other? We use the **Silver Thread** (Bridge the Divide) and the **Blue Thread** (Listen for the Unspoken) together.

Humanity Before Policy

As researchers Masullo and Duchovnay observed,[20] the "Normative Good" of democracy requires us to see the humanity in the outgroup before we bring up politics. Build the relationship first. Before you discuss the bill or proposed solution, discuss the shared pothole. Find common ground on what you both want: for children to be safe or for the community to thrive.

Listening to Understand, Not to Respond

Listening is the single most powerful tool in your blueprint. Most people in the system are listening to criticize or listening to defend. When you choose to listen to understand (**Blue Thread**), you break the trance of the reinforcing spiral.

Instead of yelling back in a comment section, ask: *"Help me understand how you reached that conclusion?"* The result is that you move the conversation from an emotional battle to a diagnostic process.

The Boundary of the Weaver

Sometimes, the most strategic move is to set a boundary. In my own life, I've had to choose not to speak to certain people about certain topics—not because I am afraid, but because I am protecting my resilience (**Pink Thread**). You cannot weave with someone who is currently trying to burn the loom. Set the boundary and stay kind.

Before you engage in a difficult conversation, ask:

Am I staying silent out of fear/insecurity, or a strategic need for peace?

Am I contributing to the *Reinforcing Spiral* by only talking to people who agree with me?

Can I verify this information before I share it?

We cannot control the media's narrative or the lies of politicians. But we *can* choose to be people who verify facts, listen with humility, and refuse to let fear dictate the weave.

The Road Less Traveled

Nonpartisanship is indeed the road less traveled, and as the poem concludes, it makes a significant difference. It is not a lack of conviction; it is a strategic choice to prioritize the mission over allegiance to any particular group. By refusing to take a side, you become the only person in the room capable of conversing with everyone. This strategic neutrality allows you to be a bridge that stands firm regardless of the political climate.

Advocacy is often a struggle, but it should never become a character assassination. We frequently demand that decision-makers listen to our stories with empathy, yet we often express our frustrations with them in hostile ways.

Ask yourself: If the words you use in private to describe those who believe differently were used to describe you publicly, how would that affect your willingness to cooperate? If you were dismissed by a policymaker simply because of your political party, you would rightfully deem it an injustice. We cannot expect the system to be bipartisan and open-minded if we are not committed to weaving with the same integrity.

By choosing nonpartisanship, you will establish a foundation of trust that transcends political divides, enabling you to build bridges with anyone, anywhere—even while listening to Bob Marley in the Sahara Desert.

The Narrative Lens: Remember the Titans

Remember the Titans is a masterclass in the **Silver Thread**. As you watch, observe how a single, unshakeable mission can act as the force that unites deeply polarized factions.

The Strategic Pivot: The film centers on a newly integrated high school football team in the 1970s. The players and the community are deeply divided by race—a "partisan" divide that threatens to destroy the team before the season even begins. Coach Boone refuses to engage in the town's politics or the external noise. Instead, he anchors the team in the mission. He forces the players to learn about one another and play for the goal, not for their "side."

The Insight: Watch for the scene at Gettysburg. Boone tells the players that if they don't find a way to come together on this "neutral" ground, they will be destroyed just as the soldiers who fought there were. He translates their personal and political conflict into a universal struggle for survival.

In advocacy, you will frequently face "Red" and "Blue" stakeholders who are hesitant to work together. This film demonstrates that maintaining neutrality and emphasizing the shared goal—the mission—can encourage opposing parties to collaborate, leading to a win-win outcome that neither could accomplish alone.

In the movie, the players stop seeing each other's race when they start seeing the jersey. In your work, the **Silver Thread** makes the mission our only "jersey." When we walk into a meeting, we don't wear a party color; we wear the mission.

The Silver Interlocks: Build Nonpartisan Bridges

A bridge requires two anchors. These interlocks ensure that your neutral stance is reinforced by integrity, allowing you to hold space for opposing sides without losing the mission's center.

Interlock	The Asset	The Stitch
Silver + Pink Maintain Resilience	Humanized Diplomacy	Anchor your peace in universal values so polarized rhetoric can't shake you.
Silver + White Maintain Humility	Neutral Convener	Remove your "jersey" at the door; the mission is the only celebrity in the room.
Silver + Yellow Learn & Unlearn	Universal Truth	Use data as a universal translator to bypass political spin.
Silver + Blue Listen for the Unspoken	Empathetic Alignment	Listen for the human *why* hidden behind partisan talking points.
Silver + Red Speak with Integrity	Unifying Call	Speak the language of the room to make your goal a win for all.
Silver + Gold Level the Loom	Bipartisan Equity	Present justice as a shared community standard rather than a political weapon.
Silver + Green Forge Alliances	Super-Coalition	Design alliances that are structurally shielded from partisan sabotage.
Silver + Gray Lead Ethically	Objective Merit	Build a reputation for fairness that outlasts election cycles.
Silver + Orange Share the Credit	Cross-Aisle Validation	Reward the bravery of crossing the aisle; value the bridge more than the credit.
Silver + Brown Act Strategically	Common-Interest Action	Fix potholes that everyone agrees are broken.
Silver + Purple Master the Pivot	Political Maneuverability	Pivot your message to stay relevant when leadership changes.

Thread Experiment: The Audit of Independence

This audit is designed to help you identify where your boundaries are made of brick and where they are made of fear. To reclaim your agency, you must learn to distinguish the mission from the fear.

Identify a policy or leader you strongly oppose.

Ask: "What am I *truly* afraid will happen if their idea succeeds?"

Trace: Am I afraid because of my own research (**Yellow**), or was I told to feel this way by a partisan news source or social media algorithm?

Find one person who supports that policy and ask them—without judgment—to explain how they believe it helps the community. Listen for the human goal buried beneath the political jargon.

Bonus Experiment

Write a one-page brief arguing—as persuasively as possible—why someone might **legitimately** oppose your goal. Look for structural or ideological reasons. If you cannot argue the opposing side's position with sincerity, you do not yet understand the system well enough to solve the problem. Once you understand their *why*, you can adjust your *how* to address their concerns before they even voice them.

Mirror Reflections

Am I rejecting expertise because the facts are wrong, or because the person delivering them doesn't wear my party's jersey?

Silver Thread Recap

You have refused to let partisanship become a mental shortcut, choosing instead to see the humanity and the *why* behind every person across the table. In doing so, you have mastered the discipline of neutrality.

The Result: Your mission is now protected by a neutral shield that prioritizes human outcomes over political agendas. Because you are willing to speak with everyone, you have earned the right to be heard by anyone.

The Anchor is Complete: Your loom is set. The vertical tension of your character—Resilience (**Pink Thread**), Humility (**White Thread**), and Neutrality (**Silver Thread**)—is now strong enough to hold the weight of the system. Without this foundation, the rest of the weave would eventually sag or snap.

It's not our differences that divide us. It's our inability to recognize, accept, and celebrate those differences.

Audre Lorde

Calibrating the Lens
Section One Conclusion

The Integrity of Vision

In photography, the lens is how you see the world. The quality and integrity of that glass are crucial; everything depends on it—including the quality of the final image. If your lens is cracked, smudged, or compromised, your image will be distorted. Even if the subject in front of you is perfect, the finished image will be flawed. In advocacy, we often blame the subject—the legislator, the stakeholder, or the system—when, in reality, it was the lens that failed to translate the truth.

In high-stress advocacy, offenses are common. If we harbor unspoken resentment, we are weaving through a cracked lens. Anything the guilty party says—even with great intentions—is viewed through that crack. You begin to read between the lines to justify your frustration. The result is that you don't see the context. You risk stalling a mission not because of a policy disagreement, but because of a hardware failure in your own perception.

Perception is Reality (Until it Isn't)

In advocacy, we move with the speed of certainty. We are fueled by our *why* and focused on our target. But perception is a hidden variable. Perception is reality for the one holding it—but perception is not **truth**. If you identify the same crack in multiple places, you haven't found a nuisance; you've found a flaw in the blueprint. Do not let the system's perception of you stop you from investigating the reality of the road.

Consider the Context: Ask questions rather than assume nefarious intent. What is this person going through? What do they know? Remember that no one is perfect—including the weaver. Offer the grace you hope to receive when your own lens is smudged.

Clear the Obstruction: Before judging the splinter in a stakeholder's eye, check the plank in your own. Is your pride hurt? Are you seeking an ego win or a mission win?

Communicate with Clarity: In-person or verbal communication is the gold standard. Digital communication (text/email) can make a minor scratch look like a total crack.

Prioritize the Repair: If the mission matters, put aside your pride to make things right. Resolve promptly; silence is where bitterness grows.

The greatest danger to an advocate is the lens of certainty. When we treat perception as an absolute stop sign, we miss the oasis of common ground; it allows us to assume they are an enemy and conversation is useless. We assume we know the plot line before we've even read the system's story. Instead, we should treat perception as a yield sign, where we can say, "I disagree with their stance, but I am curious about the story that led them there." Remembering that our lens might be cracked can help us make progress.

Life is too short and the mission is too precious to allow a blurry lens to steal our progress. Choose clarity over resentment every single time.

Now that your lens is clean and your perception is calibrated, you are ready to look at the system not as you *wish* it were, but as it actually is. It's time to gather the data.

Drafting the Pattern
Section Two

While **The Anchor** represents the heart of the system, **The Pattern** serves as its brain. This section is where your empathy intersects with evidence. If you create without data, you are simply making noise; however, when you craft with data and deep listening, you are building a compelling argument for change.

The Three Pillars of Systemic Insight:

- **Learn and Unlearn (Yellow):** Mastery of data, stakeholders, and the underlying mechanics of the system.

- **Listen for the Unspoken (Blue):** The ability to hear the unspoken fears and priorities behind a "No."

- **Speak With Integrity (Red):** The power to translate raw data into a human message that demands a solution.

Learn and Unlearn
The Yellow Thread

Background Music: The Scientist (Coldplay)

Similar to the lyrics in "The Scientist," we often find ourselves deconstructing puzzles and realizing that the "numbers and figures" of our initial assumptions don't quite add up. The Yellow Thread symbolizes the courage to return to the beginning and commit to continuous learning as our mission evolves.

Key Idea: Genuine learning involves being open to changing perspectives when new data contradicts previous assumptions; to put aside pride to unlearn old beliefs and adapt strategies to new evidence.

The most useful piece of learning for the uses of life is to unlearn what is untrue.

Antisthenes

The Power of Learning and Unlearning

The **Yellow Thread** symbolizes enlightenment, representing a disciplined commitment to continuously studying the system, the science, and the change process, as well as the courage to question your core beliefs. An advocate who follows this principle actively seeks new knowledge to ensure their message remains relevant and accurate.

This approach involves viewing each failure as an opportunity to learn and each success as a model to replicate. Such a mindset is crucial during the STUDY phase of the PDSA cycle (Plan-Do-Study-Act), where objectively analyzing results is essential—even when the data contradicts your expectations. We will explore PDSA in the **Brown Thread**.

The Socratic Method: Your Primary Tool

Learning is a journey of inquiry rather than a final destination. To navigate this journey effectively, I recommend embracing the *Socratic Method*, which involves cooperative questioning dialogues that provoke critical thinking.

> *The key to wisdom is this: constant and frequent questioning, for by questioning alone we can learn.*
>
> Socrates

In advocacy, the *Socratic Method* is your primary tool for learning and unlearning. By consistently challenging your core beliefs and the status quo, you ensure that your strategy is grounded in reality rather than mere tradition.

The Socratic Approach in Action

Instead of outright telling a stakeholder they are wrong (which often triggers defensiveness), guide them to uncover the truth:

Seek Definition: "What is the primary goal of this policy?"

Expose the Contradiction: "If the data shows [X] is happening, does that move us closer to or further from that goal?"

Guided Discovery: "Based on that, what would happen if we tried [Y] instead?"

Once a Senator or a CEO articulates the truth themselves, they will find it difficult to ignore it.

The Office Scenario

You want to move a weekly recurring meeting from Friday afternoon to Tuesday morning because the team is checked out by Friday and nothing gets done. The roadblock in this scenario is the boss: "We've always had the wrap-up meeting on Friday. It's a tradition."

Seek Definition: "I understand the tradition. If the goal of the meeting is to wrap up, what are the three most important actions we hope the team takes immediately after we finish?"

Uncover the Root: "In your experience, how many of those actions actually get started between 4:00 PM on Friday and 9:00 AM on Monday?"

Expose the Contradiction: "If the work is sitting untouched over the weekend, is the meeting acting as a 'launchpad' for the next week, or just a 'checklist' for the past one?"

Guided Discovery: "If we moved the meeting to Tuesday morning, when the team is fresh, do you think we would see more of those tasks completed by Wednesday?"

The Result: You didn't outright tell the boss that their tradition was a waste of time. Instead, you asked questions that prompted them to realize that the meeting's timing was counterproductive to its goal.

Asking questions can lead stakeholders to see things differently and even change their minds.

The Suitcase of Assumptions

As an American woman entering Tunisia, a predominantly Muslim country, I carried a suitcase full of assumptions. I expected to be disliked and was prepared for a cold reception.

I could not have been more wrong.

One afternoon, after our Arabic lessons, a friend and I entered a shop in the Souk (marketplace). We wanted to bargain for a souvenir (a local custom), so we decided to use our extremely limited and clumsy vocabulary. We stumbled over the words, probably mispronouncing nearly every syllable, and were worried we would offend him.

The shopkeeper's reaction shocked me. He wasn't insulted by our poor grammar or annoyed by our slow speaking. Instead, he was *overjoyed*. He felt appreciated because we had made the effort to try. He ended up practically giving us the item because the currency of our effort was worth more to him than the dinars in our pockets.

Just as I had assumptions about him, he had assumptions about me—that Americans are often loud, demanding, and unwilling to honor the people of the land. Our willingness to be students changed the entire dynamic of that interaction. Not only did we learn, but he also respected our *effort* to learn.

I don't remember what I bought from his shop that day, but I will never forget the shopkeeper.

The Effort is the Currency

In the world of policy and advocacy, we often feel that we can't speak up unless we have a PhD. However, the **Yellow Thread** isn't about expertise; it's about posturing.

If you walk into a legislator's office demanding they speak your language, the door will stay shut. But if you enter as a learner—asking questions and demonstrating that you've done your homework—the "shopkeeper" will open up.

To weave the **Yellow Thread** into your strategy, you must set aside your assumptions about the system.

- **Assume kindness exists in unexpected places:** If you enter expecting an enemy, you will usually find one. If you approach expecting a partner who needs to be taught about your reality, you can transform the atmosphere. Kindness and respect can be found in the cracks of even the most intimidating systems, but you must be willing to uncover them.

- **The goal is connection, not perfection:** You don't need to know every detail of the tax code or every protein strain. You need to show that you are willing to learn their "language"—the legislative process—to find a solution.

- **Be happy to be wrong:** The most powerful moments in my learning journey have been realizing that my assumptions were false. In advocacy, if you discover an unexpected ally, celebrate that. Being wrong isn't bad if your focus is on accuracy and understanding.

Facts don't require our approval.

Sharon McMahon

The Power of Unlearning

Learning involves adding new tools to your mental toolbox, but *unlearning* can be a more challenging and critical task. It requires letting go of outdated information and assumptions that are no longer true or helpful. Think of it like clearing out a cluttered closet; you need to remove the old items to make room for new ones.

For advocates, unlearning is essential since the landscapes of science, policy, and politics are constantly evolving. No matter what cause you support, the circumstances and the individuals involved are likely to change. The person you once viewed as an obstacle might turn into an ally, and the strategy you were confident would succeed may lead to a dead end.

Unlearning also requires awareness of the human tendency toward *confirmation bias*—where we actively interpret information to confirm our beliefs rather than genuinely seek the truth.[1] If we are dedicated to accuracy and letting go of untrue facts and opinions, we must avoid this.

The ability to unlearn deeply held beliefs—whether about a person, a process, or a policy—is a hallmark of a truly effective advocate.

The Reality of Learning and Unlearning

When I received my daughter's diagnosis, I immersed myself in the science, reading every study and memorizing every term. However, I soon realized that understanding the biology of the disease and its treatment options was only part of the challenge. I also needed to learn about the process of adding a condition to a newborn screening panel.

What I discovered is that advocacy is a journey of continuous learning and unlearning. My background in political science and lobbying led me to think that if a bill were well-designed and had bipartisan support, it would pass easily. Similarly, I assumed that clear scientific evidence showing that newborn screening for a specific condition was feasible and life-saving would naturally lead to its adoption. However, my experience taught me otherwise, and I had to unlearn these assumptions.

It took years to convince the advisory board of the importance of adding Krabbe disease to our panel, partly because there weren't many publications detailing recent advances at the time. This taught me how much of this process is beyond our control, but there are ways to work within the limitations.

The failure of my first two legislative attempts—both bills dying in committee—was a harsh lesson that challenged everything I thought I knew. To move forward, I had to be willing to unlearn my assumptions about the process. I didn't abandon my goal, but I adjusted my strategy to learn the unwritten rules of the system.

The Anatomy of Indifference

The greatest enemy of the **Yellow Thread** isn't just a lack of facts; it's willful ignorance. We often encounter people whose ears are sealed by pride or partisanship. They refuse to listen to expertise because a political narrative has promised them payback. However, empathy requires us to ask: "How will this impact those we love *and* those we don't?"

When a policy harms *anyone*, it eventually harms *everyone*.

True learning requires the humility to listen to those who have spent their lives solving problems for the greater good. Wisdom cannot thrive where knowledge is ignored.

The Mindset of a Learner

The foundation of your learning journey is developing the right mindset. As Adam Grant notes in his book, *Think Again,*[2] we often fall into three common modes of thinking that prevent us from learning and adapting: *Preacher Mode,* where we deliver sermons to protect our ideals; *Prosecutor*

Mode, where we try to prove others wrong; and *Politician Mode,* where we use influence to win over an audience.

These three modes directly oppose the *Scientist Mode,* which is the ideal mindset for advocacy. A scientist is actively open-minded, seeking reasons they might be *wrong,* and revising their views based on new information. This willingness to learn and adapt is crucial for long-term advocacy success.

> Thinking like a scientist involves more than just reacting with an open mind. It means being actively open-minded…revising our views based on what we learn.
>
> Adam Grant

When you walk into a meeting, ask yourself: Am I here to deliver a sermon (*Preacher*), win an argument (*Prosecutor*), or win a vote (*Politician*)? If the answer is yes to any of those, take a breath and shift to *Scientist Mode*—where you are there to find the truth.

The Parenting Scenario

Returning to the *Socratic Method,* here is another example that demonstrates these modes: Your teenager wants to stay out two hours past their curfew for a party, but they have a big game early the next morning.

The Roadblock (The Teen): "You're so unfair! Everyone else is staying late. You just don't want me to have any fun."

The Socratic Approach (The Parent):

- **Seek Definition:** "I hear that you feel this is about me stopping your fun. If we agree the goal of the curfew is to make sure you're physically ready for your game tomorrow, how much sleep do you think your body needs to play at 100%?"

- **Uncover the Root:** "If the party ends at midnight and you get home at 12:30 AM, what time would you actually be asleep?"

- **Expose the Contradiction:** "If you're asleep by 1:00 AM and have to wake up at 7:00 AM, is that the amount of rest you usually need to avoid feeling sluggish on the field?"

- **Guided Discovery:** "Since you've worked all season to start in this game, how do you think you'd feel at halftime if you only had six hours of sleep? Is there a way you can see your friends at the party but still protect the work you've put into the team?"

Why This is "Scientist Mode" for Parents

If you say "No," you are in *Preacher Mode* (protecting your rules), which triggers *Prosecutor Mode* in your child. Using the *Socratic Method* shifts you into *Scientist Mode.* You are essentially saying: *"Let's look at the data of sleep and performance together."*

The Outcome: The teenager isn't fighting *you*; they are weighing their desire for the party against their desire to play well.

The *Socratic Method* is the ultimate unlearning tool. It forces the other person to dismantle their own assumptions. Once someone says the truth out loud, they can no longer ignore it.

> **The soul of a story opens the door,**
> **but the precision of the data keeps you in the room.**

Strategic Learning

Strategic learning involves actively seeking out and connecting various pieces of information. Think of it as a chain with many links: as you engage in conversations, the knowledge you gain will help you decide whom to talk to next, bringing you one link closer to your goal.

I understand that it can be daunting to know where to start, but speaking with someone knowledgeable is often the best place to begin. And, where you begin may not be the right place, but it's a start. For me, it started with a meeting with legislative staffers who provided valuable insights on whom to approach and what to expect. Each conversation helped me build a team and strengthen my network. If someone didn't have the answer, they would connect me to someone who did.

I discovered that people were eager to support my cause and connect me to others who could help me because of the story I shared, the passion I expressed, and the clear impact I aimed to achieve. By expanding your network, you increase your chances of discovering that crucial piece of information that will guide you to the next step.

Ongoing learning and relationship-building clarify your strategy. When I began to find my path, I often felt frustrated and assumed malicious intent on the part of those who seemed to be obstructing my efforts. As I learned more about the system I was trying to change—its complexities *and* the passions of those working within it—my frustration transformed into determination and appreciation. This shift allowed me to identify and address issues more effectively, improving the system while working within it rather than against it.

Trust but Verify

In an era of engineered skepticism and rampant misinformation, information integrity is your strongest armor. This protocol is what makes you trusted in the halls of power.

The Impulse Check: When you receive information that perfectly confirms your biases, stop. Notice if you are believing it because of who said it rather than what was said.

The Source Trace: Never cite a headline. Always trace the claim back to the raw data or the primary source. If there is no citation, it is noise, not evidence.

The Pivot Practice: Normalize the phrase: "I have received new information, and I am changing my mind." In a world that prizes "doubling down," the person who can pivot based on facts is the most powerful person in the room.

Learn the Language of the Experts

In fields like public health, policy decisions are closely tied to complex science, medical ethics, and rigid bureaucratic processes. To influence outcomes effectively, you must learn the language of those who hold the power. Understanding the language of experts and the complexities of the system may take time, but it will ultimately reinforce your mission.

Master the Jargon: Familiarize yourself with the technical terms relevant to your area of policy interest. This knowledge can transform your passionate plea into a credible, technical argument.

Learn the Acronyms: The policy and public health sectors are filled with acronyms. It's crucial to understand the relevant ones, but avoid using them unless you define them first when speaking with stakeholders.

Study the Process: Understand the administrative procedures, the state's budget cycle, and the exact steps required to achieve your goals. Knowledge of the process enables you to identify new and more efficient ways to address challenges.

Know the Data: You don't need to start from scratch—investigate existing published studies and resources that can strengthen your argument. Use credible sources rather than creating new data; this saves time and reduces your workload. Whether through conversations, websites of trusted organizations, or conferences, discover where you can gather the information you need.

Advocates often worry that focusing on data might make them appear cold or disconnected from the families they serve. However, being the most informed person in the room is a sign of deep commitment. When you master the facts of the system, you can ensure that the promises you make to your community are promises the system can genuinely keep.

Humility (**White Thread**) encourages us to set aside pride, which allows us to focus on learning (**Yellow Thread**) for our benefit and the success of our objectives. Being open to strategic learning and remaining adaptable will strengthen your advocacy efforts. While you may not control the political environment, you can choose how to respond to it.

Expertise isn't an alternative to passion; it's the armor that protects it.

The Narrative Lens: The Martian

While many movies highlight the value of learning, *The Martian* takes this concept to a new level. The focus is on observing the **Yellow Thread** as a survival mechanism in a high-stakes environment.

The Strategic Pivot: Mark Watney is stranded on Mars with limited food and no hope of immediate rescue. Instead of succumbing to panic or placing blame on NASA, he shifts into "Scientist Mode." He meticulously learns the chemistry of his environment and the botany needed to grow life on a barren planet. Rather than simply wishing for more food, he audits his supplies, calculates his caloric intake, and studies the soil's composition.

The Insight: Pay attention to the moment when he calculates his caloric intake and states, "I'm going to have to science the ___ out of this." This encapsulates the idea that while passion may get you to your goal, a willingness to engage with the data is what keeps you alive and helps you succeed.

Your "soil" represents the stakeholders who have the authority to implement the changes you seek. Your "calories" are the resources at your disposal. By auditing the system and understanding the technical requirements of your objectives, you can find ways to grow your mission where others see only a barren landscape.

The Yellow Interlocks: Learn and Unlearn

Lived experience is your raw material; intelligence is the tool that shapes it. These interlocks ensure your story isn't just a moment of pain, but a piece of data.

Interlock	The Asset	The Stitch
Yellow + Pink Maintain Resilience	Curious Endurance	Frame research as a discovery mission to prevent burnout.
Yellow + White Practice Humility	Unbiased Discovery	Let "I don't know" be your most powerful tool for finding better answers.
Yellow + Silver Bridge the Divide	Universal Truth	Use data as the neutral language that stops partisan fighting in its tracks.
Yellow + Blue Listen for the Unspoken	Informed Listening	Master the jargon so you can hear the real reasons a stakeholder is saying no.
Yellow + Gray Lead Ethically	Evidence-Based Integrity	Build your case on verified facts so your ethics are never up for debate.
Yellow + Red Speak with Integrity	Credible Communication	Translate data into a human story that decision-makers can't ignore.
Yellow + Gold Level the Loom	Intellectual Equity	Use statistics to shine a light on families the system has left behind.
Yellow + Green Forge Alliances	Collaborative Intelligence	Share your homework with your allies to raise the coalition's IQ.
Yellow + Orange Share the Credit	Validated Success	Use measurable metrics to prove your mission works, earning more momentum.
Yellow + Brown Act Strategically	Validated Velocity	Ensure every action is backed by evidence to avoid wasted effort.
Yellow + Purple Master the Pivot	Intelligent Agility	Use new information as a "green light" to pivot your strategy instantly.

Thread Experiments: The Source Check

The Task: Take a fact you frequently use and trace it back to its primary source (the original study or data set). Is this information accurate?

The Mastery: Credibility is your most valuable asset. By verifying your foundation, you ensure that your mission is built on solid ground rather than on rumors. In a world filled with misinformation and disinformation, accuracy is essential.

Bonus Experiments:

Set aside an hour this week to formally research a specific challenge you are currently facing. Your output should be a one-page, jargon-free summary of the problem, the current process in place, and the person with the authority to make a change.

Dedicate fifteen minutes this week to reading a new scientific study or policy change related to your cause. Summarize it into one simple paragraph for your community.

Mirror Reflections

Am I dismissing expertise because the facts are incorrect, or because the person presenting them does not align with my beliefs? If I were presented with this data as an impartial fact, would it change my mind, or is it meant to confirm my existing beliefs?

Yellow Thread Recap

You have traded guesses for data, committing to the rigorous research required to understand the technical blueprint of the problem.

The Result: You are now a technical partner to the system, possessing the expertise that earns a seat at the decision-making table.

The Next Stitch: Now that you have mastered the facts, we move to the **Blue Thread**, where we learn to listen for the unspoken rules, motives, and constraints that data alone cannot reveal.

It's what we think we already know that often prevents us from learning.

Claude Bernard

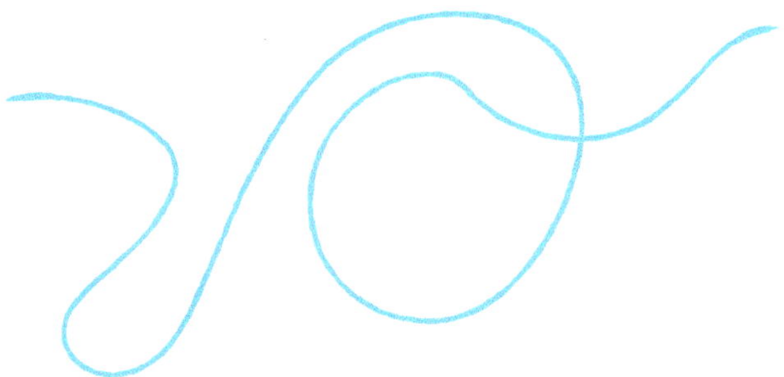

Listen for the Unspoken
The Blue Thread

Background Music: We Can Work It Out (The Beatles)

Perspective serves as a critical bridge in advocacy. This song highlights the tension of the Blue Thread: the understanding that insisting on seeing things "our way" alone can jeopardize the mission. Active empathy is essential, as it can turn a stakeholder's anxiety into a strategic breakthrough.

Key Idea: Listening to understand,[1] rather than simply to respond, is the first and most important step in effective advocacy. It involves setting aside your agenda and biases to fully grasp others' perspectives, motivations, and underlying emotions. This approach is vital for building empathy, fostering trust, and identifying common ground.

Listening to understand doesn't obligate us to agree.

Sharon McMahon

Listen to Understand, Not to Reply

Continuous learning and unlearning (**Yellow Thread**) are essential for gathering objective data and scientific truth. However, facts alone cannot solve systemic problems. To effectively apply this knowledge, you must master a powerful yet often-overlooked skill in advocacy: listening to understand. This crucial step involves setting aside your own agenda to identify the human and systemic obstacles that hinder change.

> *Listening to understand requires humility, a willingness to be wrong, and the ability to change one's mind when new information is obtained. It humanizes those on the other side and helps better understand the motivations behind their stance.*[2]
>
> Bud Bilanich

As Mónica Guzmán said, "connecting with other humans is what makes our lives rich and meaningful. Especially when so much can pull us apart."[3] The beauty of listening to different perspectives is that they often come from vastly different lived experiences and contain wisdom we might not otherwise encounter. We can then take the perspectives from those with whom we connect and change policy to make life better without having to endure those problems ourselves. That's why we have so openly shared our story about Tori—to affect change so that our story doesn't have to be someone else's. We try to use our pain to reduce the pain of others.

Listening to understand and being willing to humbly learn can change us as people. And it can truly change the world. But that doesn't mean it's easy or comfortable.

The Root of the Rushed Solution

During my time in Haiti, we received a directive that felt both liberating and terrifying: "Walk through the community and do whatever you feel led to do." As a strategist, I didn't like that. I wanted specific instructions and a map. However, when you are in a landscape of rubble, the most important work isn't found on a map; it's uncovered in the "boring" details of a conversation.

Living in the Rubble (Port-au-Prince, 2010)

As we walked through the neighborhood, we met a man who was battling tuberculosis. He had the life-saving antibiotics provided by an NGO, but he wasn't taking them. From a distance, a policy-maker might look at this situation and say, "We have a compliance issue. We need a campaign to educate him on why taking medicine is important."

But we sat down with him and listened.

I discovered that he wasn't "non-compliant" at all—he was hungry. The medicine was so strong that it made him violently ill if taken on an empty stomach, and he had no food. I happened to have a small bag of crackers in my backpack. In that situation, a fifty-cent bag of crackers meant more than a million-dollar pharmaceutical budget.

You may have noticed this, too: people often assume they know what is needed without consulting those with the relevant expertise. As a result, problems remain unresolved because we fail to listen.

Why does this happen? Whether it's conducting disaster relief efforts in Haiti or pushing through a bill that fails to address the real issues, we tend to prefer the fixer approach. We want to be the ones with the answers and the ones who arrive with pre-drawn blueprints.

At the root of this tendency is pride. We can become so enamored with our version of the skyscraper that we ignore the input of those on the ground—the very people who may be falling into the potholes—who are telling us that the foundation is shaky.

> Learning how to sit with the discomfort of what I don't understand opened my life. It's okay to sit down and listen. To de-center our own opinions. And learn what we do not know.
>
> Tia Levings

Strategy Without Sight

Listening is not a sign of weakness; it is the highest form of strategic intelligence. We often think we are listening when we are merely waiting for our turn to speak. We arrive with our grand solutions and are baffled when they don't work. In Haiti, I witnessed well-meaning organizations spending millions on projects that the community neither needed nor could sustain. They brought the *what,* but they never took the time to ask the residents who actually live there about the *why* or *how.*

True listening is the act of asking, *what are we missing?*

Stop solving, start sifting: Rather than entering a meeting with a predetermined answer, come equipped with a sieve. Sift through the distractions until you discover the "cracker"—the specific reason why a legislator is saying no or why a family cannot access a clinic.

Listen for the *why*: If a system isn't working, there is likely a pothole you haven't identified yet. Is it a lack of transportation? A fear of losing another benefit? Or perhaps crackers?

The smallest detail is often the lever: In Haiti, food was the lever. In your state, it might be a single line of code in an insurance database. You won't find this lever until you stop talking and start observing the mechanics of the struggle.

The **Blue Thread** taught me that I didn't need a grand policy to change someone's day; I just needed to listen to what his stomach was telling him. In your advocacy work, the most powerful action you can take is to find the "cracker" that allows the medicine to work effectively.

Beyond Hearing Words

Effective advocacy requires a significant shift in focus. It's not just about sharing your side of the story; it's also about listening to the experiences that shape others' views.

When I began advocating, I was a grieving mother, driven by strong emotions, who didn't realize how crucial it was to listen to those with in-depth system knowledge. Often, I ended discussions feeling discouraged, mistakenly believing that unanswered questions were obstacles. Only later did I recognize that stakeholders were seeking specific information to help me; I just wasn't providing it. I had to listen to *them* with the same attention I wanted them to extend to me.

The foundation of humility, which prepares us for this vital step, is essential. Listening to understand is an act of humility *and* courage. It means setting aside your grief-fueled assumptions and biases to fully comprehend others' perspectives, motivations, and underlying emotions. This is the crucial step in finding common ground. When you approach discussions with a genuine curiosity, you are prepared to gather the information needed to fix systemic potholes, build alliances, and create lasting change. This process involves moving beyond simply waiting for your turn to speak and genuinely engaging with the worldviews of those you aim to influence.

> To be an activist is to speak. To be an advocate is to listen. Society can't move forward without both.
>
> Eva Marie Lewis

Diagnosing Before You Prescribe

In medicine, a doctor who prescribes surgery before conducting a diagnostic test is considered negligent. Similarly, someone who demands a bill before understanding the system is ineffective. In my personal experience with newborn screening, well-meaning advocates often rush to initiate legislation to add a condition to their state's panel, even though every state has a process that rarely requires legislation. Listening to understand helps you distinguish between a solid barrier and a hurdle, making the journey easier to navigate.

You cannot re-engineer a system until you have truly heard the people who run it.

It is worth noting that *listening to understand* is different than *active listening*, which can often be performative.[4] When you're seeking to diagnose problems, listen to understand.

Another way to describe this practice is *empathic listening,* which is a profound way to connect with others. When you listen with empathy, you're not just preparing your response; you're building a bridge.[5] This process not only helps you gather essential information but also makes the person speaking feel heard and respected, transforming a potential adversary into a valuable resource.

A lack of empathic listening can lead to significant setbacks. Imagine an advocate filled with frustration who spends a meeting making demands without ever inquiring about the official's knowledge or perspective. As a result, both parties leave feeling defensive and unheard.

Now, consider a different approach. The advocate shares their personal story and then asks a strategic question: "What are the biggest challenges you face when considering changes to the program?" This approach helps the official feel respected, shifting the conversation from a list of demands to a collaborative problem-solving session. This principle encourages you to "diagnose before you prescribe."

Personal Experience with Listening to Understand

My advocacy journey began in a conference room just three weeks after my daughter's death. Driven by grief, I attended a Newborn Screening Advisory Board meeting with a single, uncompromising goal: to get Pennsylvania to screen for Krabbe disease. However, by truly listening over several meetings, I began to understand that the problem was far more complex than a single disease or decision.

My breakthrough came when the board chair, frustrated with the stagnant system, asked, "Why are we even here?" This was in response to learning that the legislature had denied a request for a budget increase to add a condition to the state's panel. He raised a valid point: why were these dedicated experts volunteering their time and energy to recommend conditions only to be repeatedly blocked by those who didn't understand the science or the stakes involved?

In that moment, I realized I heard more than just a question; it was a clear indication that my fight wasn't against a specific denial but against a broken system. I had misdiagnosed the problem, but I now knew what to fix.

This experience taught me that true, lasting advocacy begins with listening for systemic potholes—the points of failure that create frustration for everyone involved. It also became clear to me that science often moves faster than bureaucracy, a problem few of us can solve.

As someone new to this landscape, I noticed these potholes more easily, as those deeply involved had become accustomed to the existing problems. My fresh perspective—the ability to see the system as a stakeholder rather than just a grieving parent—was a crucial contribution I could bring to the table.

The Architecture of a Worldview

In recent years, I have had numerous encounters with people who unknowingly taught me valuable lessons about truly listening to other perspectives.

One was a fellow mom I met at a local gathering. On the surface, we could not have been more different—or so I assumed. Based on her appearance and interests, my partisan lens told me she was an adversary. But through honest, patient conversations over the course of a few months, I realized I was looking at a label when I should have been looking at a person. It was through her that I learned the value of the most dangerous question an advocate can ask: *"What if I'm wrong?"*

By listening to understand rather than to reply, I saw the humanity behind her position. I felt the calmness behind her stance and discovered the story that led her to her values. And I even changed my mind on a few things.

We all have a story. What matters most is whether you are truly interested in the story of those you consider your enemies or not.

The second arrived during a tumultuous time in our country, right as I was beginning to question my own partisanship. A friend lived with us for a season, and we spent hours in conversation. I expected anger or a desire to "ruin the country"—the very things my former party leaders insisted the "other side" wanted.

Instead, I found evidence. I found a person who knew things I did not, who could articulate his reasoning with facts rather than vitriol. He held his worldview loosely enough to change it when presented with new information. He taught me to ask myself, *what am I missing?*

How many of us struggle with that? It is easier to stick with what we've been told to believe, even when the blueprint is clearly flawed. *What are the consequences of being wrong, but holding onto a belief out of pride?*

Applying The Blue Thread to Advocacy

Lasting change comes from understanding and addressing the small, specific potholes within a system, and you can only identify these roadblocks by listening carefully to those who work in the system every day.

In the **Silver Thread,** I mentioned the idea of *connectivity* and its essential role in both democracy and advocacy. One of the principles of *connective democracy* is "people must see the humanity of the other side by spending time together." [6] If we do not interact with those we consider to be adversaries, we are less likely to see them as human and therefore less likely to truly listen to their viewpoints.[7]

When we silo ourselves into groups that think like us, it becomes easier for a *them* to emerge, and easier for us to prefer comfort over curiosity. Whether online or in real life, when we refuse to put ourselves in situations where we interact with those who see things differently, it becomes impossible to listen to understand.

In my own life, this skill has been both challenging and rewarding. I find that the more curious I choose to become, the more I want to learn. The more I learn, the more curious I become. Kate Murphy's research confirms that "Listening requires, more than anything, curiosity." [8]

Listening to understand is a skill that requires practice. It is not simply waiting for your turn to speak; it requires curiosity and a willingness to comprehend what someone is expressing and why. You do not have to agree with them,[9] but it is essential to listen meaningfully so that you can understand their perspective and respond appropriately. By listening to those familiar with the system, you are more likely to discover effective solutions.

A strategic advocate understands that:

- In a meeting, they **listen more than they speak**. They ask open-ended questions and pay close attention to uncover shared interests or hidden roadblocks.

- They listen not only for facts but also for the emotions and motivations behind the words, which helps them tailor their message. They can turn a skeptic into an ally by first listening to their concerns and then addressing them with respect and data.

- **It is always possible for minds to change, even when it seems impossible.**

I have learned that I can work with my enemies, because they might have a change of heart at any moment.

Septima Clark

The Advocate's Toolkit: Why Theory Matters

The chart below provides brief descriptions of *Framing Theory*,[10] *Narrative Paradigm Theory*,[11] *Situational Theory of Publics*,[12] *Social Judgment Theory*,[13],[14] *Agenda-Setting Theory*,[15] and *Systems Theory*.[16]

Here's how we utilize these tools to build bridges:

Framing Theory	How you package information determines how people feel about it. If you tell a legislator, "This program costs $1 million," they see an enormous expense. If you frame it as, "This program saves $10 million in future ER visits," they see an investment. You aren't changing the facts; you are choosing which part of the facts to put in the frame.
Narrative Paradigm Theory	People aren't moved by spreadsheets; they are moved by stories. This theory suggests that humans are natural storytellers and therefore respond better to stories. You can show a graph of disease progression, but when you tell the story of how your daughter was never able to walk, you create a Narrative. A good story has fidelity—it rings true to the human heart. Use yours to make the data stick.
Situational Theory of Publics	People ignore things that don't feel personal. The goal is to move publics from being **Latent** (asleep) to **Aware** (looking) to **Active** (doing). A neighbor might not care about Newborn Screening until you explain how it impacts the local hospital where their grandkids were born. Find the hook that makes your cause pertain to them.
Social Judgment Theory	We all have a Latitude of Acceptance. If your request is too far outside someone's beliefs, they will reject it instantly. If you ask a fiscal conservative for a massive new government agency, they'll say no. If you ask them to fix a specific pothole in an existing agency, you are within their Latitude of Acceptance. Listen first to find where their comfort zone is, then park your request right inside the lines.
Agenda-Setting Theory	The media doesn't tell people what to think, but it tells them what to think about. If you get three local news stories about your cause in one month, the local representative will suddenly find it top of mind during their next session. Consistent noise creates priority.
Systems Theory	Every part of a system is connected to the others. If you pull one thread, the whole web moves. Adding a condition to a screening panel isn't just a medical decision; it affects state labs, insurance companies, and hospitals. Use communication to connect the dots. You are the "nerve center" that connects the different parts of the system.

In communication, the art of listening is essential, as is the study of communication theory. I know—*theory* might sound like a tedious lecture in a dusty classroom. However, in *Strategic Communication*, my graduate area of focus, theory serves as your GPS. It's the difference between shouting into the wind and having a conversation that truly resonates with someone. Essentially, *Strategic Communication* is the art of delivering the right message at the right time, through the right messenger. These theories are not just for academics; they provide "X-ray vision." When you listen to a stakeholder, you aren't just hearing words—you are also listening for the frame they use and the public they represent. This understanding is key to communicating strategically.

By keeping these concepts in mind, you are prepared to listen strategically—taking into account the speaker and their place in the system you are trying to change.

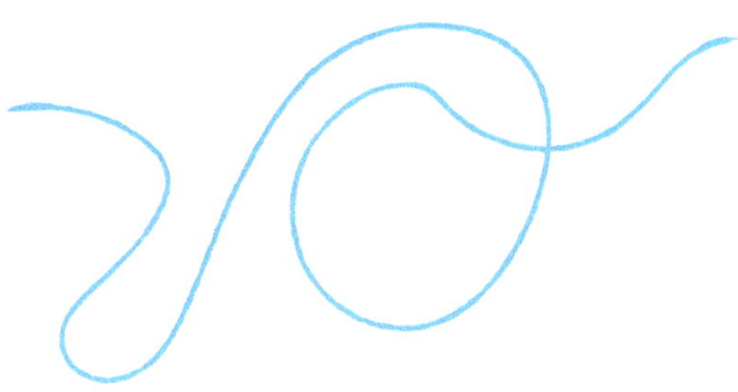

Be curious, not judgmental.

Ted Lasso

Three Dimensions of Strategic Listening[17]

Political Listening: When you speak to a legislator or their staff, listen not for what they can do for you, but for what their current priorities are. For example, if the legislator mentions "taxpayer burden," your next communication should directly relate the low cost of your proposed change to the high cost of lifelong care, demonstrating the relevance of your issue to their priorities.

Bureaucratic Listening: Bureaucracy is inherently risk-averse. Listen for specific fears: Is it, "We don't have the money," or "We don't have the personnel?" Identifying the exact fear allows you to tailor a S.M.A.R.T. action (**Brown**) to address that particular concern. Your response should focus on how other states have successfully resolved similar issues rather than arguing the science.

Empathic Listening: Even the best scientific evidence needs public support. You must listen carefully to the concerns of the general public and advocacy partners, and address them proactively before they become a barrier to your goals.

I learned early on that passionate people love to feel heard; people who feel heard are more likely to help you.

Be the type of person they want to help.

The Narrative Lens: The Devil Wears Prada

A movie that perfectly illustrates the power of observation is *The Devil Wears Prada*. If you aren't familiar with it, I'd encourage you to watch it through a strategic lens. The goal is to observe the **Blue Thread** as a requirement for decoding a powerful culture's "Internal Logic" before attempting to influence it.

The Strategic Pivot: Andy Sachs enters the high-stakes world of fashion with a *Prosecutor* mindset—judging the industry as shallow and irrelevant. Because she doesn't listen to the nuances of why things are done a certain way, she fails repeatedly. The pivot happens when she stops judging and starts observing. She learns the history, the vocabulary, and the logic behind the decisions.

The cerulean speech represents the moment Andy realizes that even things she thought were accidental (like a blue sweater) were actually the result of a highly disciplined system. In advocacy, the cerulean moment is when you realize a *no* from a lab isn't a lack of compassion—it's a response to a specific barrier you didn't know existed.

The Insight: Watch for the moment Andy stops rolling her eyes and starts asking, "What do I need to know?" In advocacy, we often walk into rooms that feel uncomfortable and unfamiliar. If we judge the system before we decode it, we remain outsiders. But when we use the **Blue Thread** to understand their pressures and their language, we find the key to moving the mission forward.

The Blue Interlocks: Listen to Understand

Effective advocacy begins in the silence. These interlocks ensure you aren't just hearing words, but decoding the *why* behind the system's "no." Strategic listening isn't passivity; it's an act of intelligence.

Interlock	The Asset	The Stitch
Blue + Pink Maintain Resilience	Relational Resilience	Listen to critics without taking it personally; use their feedback to toughen your skin.
Blue + White Practice Humility	Deep Receptivity	Silence your internal rebuttal generator to truly hear what the system needs.
Blue + Silver Bridge the Divide	Empathetic Alignment	Listen for the *why* buried beneath the partisan talking points.
Blue + Yellow Learn & Unlearn	Informed Listening	Use your technical knowledge to catch the nuance in an expert's hesitation.
Blue + Gray Lead Ethically	Evaluative Integrity	Listen for the truth, even when it's uncomfortable or challenges your current plan.
Blue + Red Speak with Integrity	Responsive Messaging	Adapt your words based on the feedback you hear in real-time.
Blue + Gold Level the Loom	Equitable Listening	Give the loudest voice to those who have been historically silenced by the system.
Blue + Green Forge Alliances	Coalitional Empathy	Understand your partners' "win conditions" so the alliance stays strong.
Blue + Orange Share the Credit	Feedback Momentum	Use community feedback to prove you are listening, which fuels trust and speed.
Blue + Brown Act Strategically	Actionable Insights	Only take action once you have truly heard the pothole's history.
Blue + Purple Master the Pivot	Strategic Pivot	Use a stakeholder's "No" as the data point that tells you exactly where to pivot.

Thread Experiments: Wait for the "And"

The Task: In your next conversation, when the other person finishes speaking, count to five or ten in your head before responding.

The Mastery: The most vital information is often hidden in the silence. By giving others space, you allow them time to reveal the internal logic you need to solve the problem.[18]

Bonus Experiment:

Identify someone in your life who holds different beliefs on any topic, and engage in a sincere conversation. Approach the discussion with curiosity by asking questions to understand their viewpoint and be open to changing your perspective. You might discover you have more in common than you think.

A very helpful book for this process is *"I Never Thought of It That Way"* by Mónica Guzmán.[19]

Mirror Reflection

If someone says something that angers you or if you see a decision that frustrates you, approach the situation with curiosity. Ask yourself: What don't I know? What am I missing? Who might be able to help me understand? Give the benefit of the doubt instead of assuming malicious intent.

Blue Thread Recap

You have moved beyond hearing to diagnostic listening, uncovering the *why* behind the system's friction and the humanity behind your adversary's stance.

The Result: You are no longer merely hearing words but decoding motivations, transforming potential adversaries into collaborative allies.

The Next Stitch: Now that you have the data and the context, we move to the **Red Thread**, where we learn the art of strategic framing—translating your intelligence into a narrative that moves people to action.

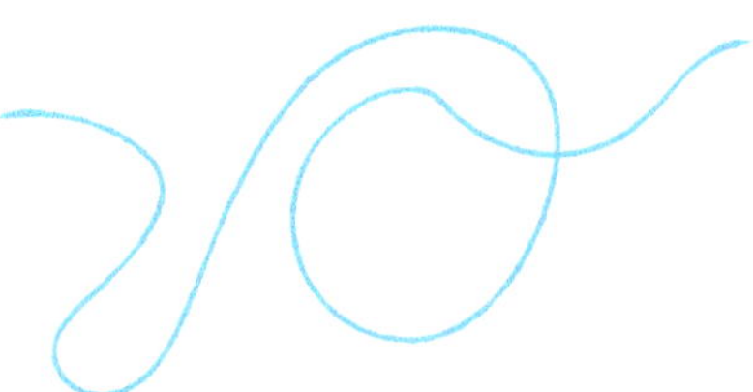

Argue like you're right and listen like you're wrong.

Adam Grant

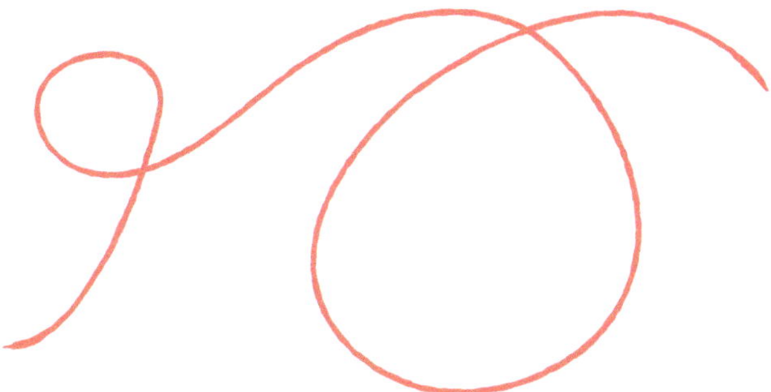

Speak with Integrity
The Red Thread

Background Music: I Won't Back Down (Tom Petty)

Clarity is your greatest asset. Once you have used the Yellow and Blue threads to uncover the truth, your communication must become non-negotiable. This song represents the moment your personal story and your data merge into a message that cannot be swayed by political pressure. "I won't back down" is not an act of aggression; it's an act of truth. When your message is built on data and empathy, standing your ground becomes a service to the mission.

Key Idea: Strategic communication isn't just about being heard; it's about being understood by those who have the power to say yes.

If it is not right, do not do it; if it is not true, do not say it.
Marcus Aurelius

Fact Meets Feeling: The Science of Persuasion

Listening to understand a stakeholder's priorities is only the first part of the strategy. To drive change, you must transform those insights into a compelling message that demands attention. The **Red Thread** serves as the active force of translation—taking the complex data of your cause and turning it into a clear, compelling truth. It's the strategic art of converting your personal story and complex data into a clear, unassailable message that moves a listener's empathy toward specific, urgent action.

Communication is not merely about conveying information; it's about translating your truth so it is both **heard and understood.**

For months, I shared my story with the raw emotion of a parent who had just experienced trauma. I wanted my anger and pain to motivate people to act. However, I quickly realized that while emotion is powerful, it can also be overwhelming for both the listener and me. I needed to distill my story into a clear, concise message that could be heard and acted upon. I had to learn to speak not only with a parent's heart but also with data to support my message.

As **W. Edward Deming** famously stated, *"Without data, you're just another person with an opinion."* Data lends credibility, supports your claims, and turns anecdotal experiences into convincing evidence. However, the most effective advocacy messages blend personal stories with robust data. As Brené Brown noted, *"Maybe stories are just data with a soul."*[1]

To persuade others effectively, it is essential to understand their core values and beliefs, which influence their perspectives on the topic. For instance, political party affiliation can affect their views and even their choice of words. Recognizing what to say and what to avoid with a particular audience is crucial.

Vulnerability as Impact

Many people believe that appearing strong or unshakable is crucial for influence. However, there is a connection between vulnerability and impact.

In recent years, our neighbors lost three large, shade-giving trees. While they weren't my trees, I immediately felt their absence; our yard became warmer, and our shade-loving plants began to wither because they were now vulnerable to the strength of the afternoon sun.

In advocacy, you are the trees. Personal loss—your vulnerability—affects the entire ecosystem. When you share your authentic, messy self, you provide shade for others. You offer a reprieve to those who are suffering through the same challenges you have faced.

Being vulnerable is not a weakness; it is a strength. Changing your mind when presented with new information isn't flip-flopping; rather, it represents the ultimate form of integrity. When we learn more, we must strive to do better.

> The story is the shortest distance
> between a human being and the truth.
>
> Anthony de Mello

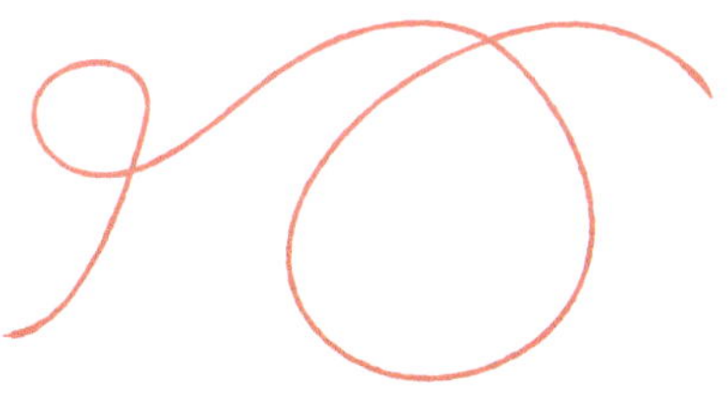

Applying the Red Thread to Advocacy

While your personal story carries weight, it needs to be backed by facts to establish credibility. Engaging with officials, legislators, or the public requires you to leverage your integrity as your most important asset.

Your story is what happened to you, and it's the spark behind your advocacy; a **narrative** is why it matters to everyone else and it is the fuel that keeps the fire burning. If we only share our grief, people might feel bad, but they won't know how to help. We don't want them to carry our burden; we want them to help us fix the road.

The **Red Thread** emphasizes the importance of supporting your emotional narrative with accurate data. Being honest about the challenges and demonstrating your understanding of the issue will help foster trust and position you as a reliable voice in the conversation. When we combine our narrative with data, we do more than appeal to emotions; we ensure that stakeholders recognize that one may not fully comprehend a proposed solution unless they've experienced the problem firsthand. Your participation in discussions helps ensure that the solution reflects the real challenges faced by those it aims to serve.

Building Your Plan

As you create a plan, it can be overwhelming because the options for communication are nearly endless. Blog posts, op-eds, social media reels, and patient story videos can all effectively convey your message. By narrowing down the who, why, what, and when, the how will become clearer.

Communicate as you would want others to communicate with you. While passion and emotion are important, speaking with integrity must include kindness and respect. Being assertive doesn't mean being disrespectful.

> ## Questions to guide every communication:
>
> **The Audience:** Who is the only person who can say "Yes"?
> **The Anchor:** What is the one **Yellow** fact they cannot argue with?
> **The Heart:** What is the one **Blue** story that proves the human cost?
> **The Frame:** Are you using their language?
> **The Ask:** Is your request a skyscraper (too big) or a pothole (actionable today)?

Framing and Reframing

To engage stakeholders in your cause, it's essential to convey the *why* of the issue before you present the *what now*. For instance, when I discuss expanding newborn screening panels with stakeholders, I begin with the day my daughter was diagnosed. I share the horror I felt upon learning that we could do nothing to help her because we were too late. Then, I illustrate how the situation might have been different had she been diagnosed at birth through newborn screening. This approach demonstrates the problem and prompts stakeholders to consider how to solve it. By providing this meaningful context, you effectively frame the issue and underscore the need for their involvement, thereby increasing their receptiveness to your proposed solutions.

A strategic advocate never defends someone else's frame. If you argue within their parameters, you risk losing ground. Instead, pivot to a frame that positions your solution as the most logical choice.

Reframing "Stress"

I have sat in countless rooms filled with technical experts—people who manage risk, budgets, and administrative rules. My least favorite objection to adding conditions is the idea of *undue stress*. While I logically understand not stressing parents out unnecessarily, to some, it is a data point to be avoided at the cost of the screening itself.

This phrase admittedly makes me angry because of my loss. Now, I redefine the phrase entirely: *You are defining undue stress as the temporary anxiety of a parent waiting for a test result. I am defining it as the lifelong, permanent trauma of a mother discovering she could have saved her child, but couldn't, because she was too late. We can manage the stress of a test; we cannot manage the stress of a funeral.*

The first time I offered this response, the room went silent. I had taken their strongest objection and turned it into my most unassailable argument. I had moved the conversation from a medical *may* to a moral *must.* I wasn't just a mom in a hallway anymore; I was redefining the terms of the trade.

Here is another example of reframing:

The Objection: "We can't install a fence around the park; it's an eyesore and makes the neighborhood look like a construction zone."

The Pivot: "I agree that preserving the aesthetic of our park is important. However, the current issue is one of liability—we've had three close calls with toddlers and the nearby street this month. By using a decorative 'living fence' of hedges, we aren't just adding a barrier; we are **investing in a safety standard** that protects our children."

In the example above, the advocate did three things:

Validated the concern: I agree.

Challenged the definition: The current issue is liability.

Introduced the new value: Safety standard.

When you speak with integrity, you realize that you aren't fighting people; you are addressing limiting perspectives. When you understand the specific concern they have, address it in your opening narrative by reframing that concern. Once you change the frame, the eyesore fence becomes a protection.[2]

How to Apply This to Your Cause

Identify the Term: Focus on a specific challenge (e.g., cost or stress).

Challenge the Definition: Examine whether their definition of risk considers the consequences of inaction.

Invite them into the Shoes: Ask questions that encourage others to view the issue from the perspective of those affected.

Years of learning (**Yellow Thread**) and listening (**Blue Thread**) have taught me to anticipate their hesitations and counter their objections before they even voice them. While I may still feel anger, I strive to stay five moves ahead.

It's essential to recognize that if they have not personally experienced the issue we are trying to address, they are more likely to object or resist taking action. Put yourself in their position: would you care?

A strategic advocate must be ready to counter common objections and shift the conversation from a moral argument to one about budgetary or logistical concerns. Your role is to pivot their focus and invite them to collaborate in solving the problem by using the "So What?" filter.

The "So What?" Filter

To ensure your signal is high-fidelity, every communication must pass the **"So What?" Filter.** Imagine a busy lawmaker looking at your slide deck or your email and asking, *"So what? Why does this matter to me right now?"*

The Story (Blue) gets them to stop walking.

The Data (Yellow) gets them to start listening.

The Frame (Red) gets them to say yes.

The Currency of Advocacy

The effectiveness of your communication is intrinsically linked to your integrity. In the halls of a state Capitol or at a community meeting, your credibility is your most valuable asset—it is the only currency you have, and it must be protected at all costs. A strategic advocate doesn't just speak; they communicate based on a foundation of trust. This means consistently being:

Transparent: Never exaggerate facts or mislead stakeholders to get a win. A single debunked statistic can dismantle years of work.

Constructive: Don't just point out what is broken. Focus on solutions that benefit the entire community.

Collaborative: Share information with fellow advocates. Collective success is more sustainable than solo victories.

When you combine high-level communication skills with unshakeable integrity, your role shifts. You stop being a complainer and begin acting as a systemic consultant.

> **The most powerful ask is the one
> that requires no translation.**

A strategic advocate:

- **Uses personal stories as evidence:** You use your experiences to provide both credibility and urgency.

- **Frames the systemic problem:** Shift the focus from your individual struggle to the larger pothole that affects everyone.

- **Translates the jargon:** Break down complex medical or legal terms into simple, compelling truths that anyone can understand.

- **Pivots with precision:** Be prepared to counter objections by immediately redirecting the conversation back to the fiscal and ethical imperative for action.

When you maintain 100% accuracy—even when the truth is complicated—you become unassailable. Stakeholders will start coming to you for information because they know you won't spin the data. Integrity is the armor that protects your mission from political pushback.

The Narrative Lens: Legally Blonde

Legally Blonde is the first movie that comes to mind when discussing the importance of strategic communication. As you watch, pay attention to the **Red Thread** and the power of a message that the rest of the world underestimates.

The Strategic Pivot: When Elle Woods enters Harvard Law, she is widely dismissed because she doesn't "look the part." The professors and her peers treat her as a joke. However, Elle doesn't change her identity to fit in; instead, she sharpens her communication. She recognizes that her unique perspective—based on her life experiences—provides insights into the case that the traditional experts overlook.

The Insight: Observe the courtroom scene where Elle wins the case by leveraging her specialized knowledge of hair-care maintenance (the Perm scene). This moment is a masterclass in **Red Thread** Communication: she takes her personal narrative, anchors it in technical facts (**Yellow Thread**), and delivers a powerful point that demolishes the opposition's argument.

In advocacy, people may underestimate you because you don't look like a lobbyist. This film demonstrates that your unique story can be your greatest asset. When you communicate authentically and back it up with sharp, technical precision, you can succeed in environments where you may have felt unwelcome.

The Red Interlocks: Speak with Integrity

Adjusting your pitch for different audiences isn't an act of manipulation—it is an act of respect. It shows that you care enough about the outcome to express your mission in a language the system speaks.

Interlock	The Asset	The Stitch
Red + Pink Maintain Resilience	Resilient Rhetoric	Speak from a place of hope and wellness, not frantic burnout.
Red + White Practice Humility	Authentic Voice	Keep the *why* bigger than the "Me" to build instant trust.
Red + Silver Bridge the Divide	The Unifying Call	Use "bilingual" language to make your cause a universal necessity.
Red + Yellow Learn & Unlearn	Evidentiary Impact	Use your data as the skeleton that holds up the heart of your story.
Red + Blue Listen for the Unspoken	Resonant Framing	Listen for their keywords so you can mirror their values.
Red + Gray Lead Ethically	Unassailable Advocacy	Refuse to exaggerate; let the truth be your most powerful tool.
Red + Gold Level the Loom	The Equity Lens	Use your microphone to make the invisible disparities visible.
Red + Green Forge Alliances	The Unified Voice	Coordinate the message so the whole alliance speaks as one.
Red + Orange Share the Credit	Amplified Impact	Give credit away to make the movement's volume even louder.
Red + Brown Act Strategically	The Directive Ask	Always end with a specific, easy-to-do next step.
Red + Purple Master the Pivot	Narrative Agility	Drop the script and pivot the pitch the moment you lose the room.

Thread Experiments: The Napkin Pitch

The Task: Explain your mission or a specific bill to a friend using only one sentence and avoiding jargon.

The Mastery: If you can explain it clearly on a napkin, you can create significant change.

Bonus Experiments

Identify one local reporter who covers your cause or policy in general. Draft a tailored, one-paragraph pitch that frames your personal story as evidence of a systemic problem that requires urgent public attention.

Develop a *Hallway Hook*: a fifteen-second statement that stops a busy stakeholder in their tracks. It isn't a summary of the ask; it's a summary of the urgency. For example: "Every month we wait to add this condition, another child in Pennsylvania loses the window for treatment."

Mirror Reflection

If you heard the story you are telling for the first time while walking through a crowded airport, would it make you stop—or would you keep walking?

Red Thread Recap

You have stripped away the jargon and the noise, choosing instead to frame your mission through the values and language of the room you are in. You have mastered the art of **Strategic Framing**.

The Result: Your message is no longer just a story; it is a clear, actionable directive that is heard rather than just listened to.

The Next Stitch: The Pattern is now interlocked with **The Anchor**. You have established who you are (your character) and mapped what you are up against. The blueprint is technically sound, but a blueprint sitting on a desk cannot build a skyscraper. It needs a crew. We now move from the architect's desk to the communal loom. We transition from Strategic Intelligence to Social Influence.

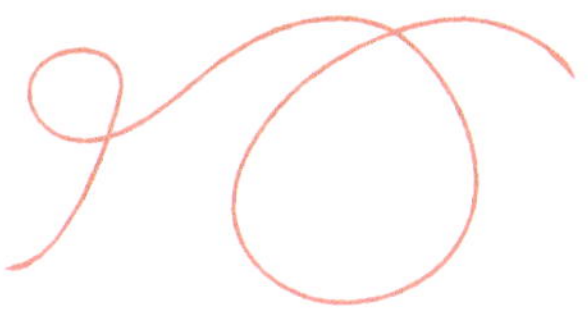

The art of advocacy is to lead you
to my conclusion on your terms.

Adam Grant

Calibrating the Signal
Section Two Conclusion

You have spent this section in the laboratory of the system. You have mined the data (**Yellow Thread**), practiced diagnostic listening (**Blue Thread**), and translated your experience into a strategic frame (**Red Thread**).

But information, on its own, is just noise.

In a legislative office or a boardroom, decision-makers are bombarded with "noise"—endless requests, conflicting data, and emotional pleas. If your message is just another sound in the room, it will be filtered out by the system's natural defenses. To be an effective advocate, you must calibrate your message until it is a **clear, sharp signal.**

The Science of Unlearning

The hardest part of drafting your pattern isn't what you learn; it's what you are willing to unlearn. We often enter a mission with "facts" that are actually just feelings we've held for a long time.

Calibration requires the integrity to take a pin to your own bubble. If the data (**Yellow Thread**) proves your assumption was wrong, do you have the courage to change your mind? An accurate blueprint is more valuable than a comfortable lie. Integrity means refusing to spin the data—if you exaggerate a statistic for a quick win, you introduce a flaw that could eventually bring the whole structure down.

The Human Frequency

Listening (**Blue Thread**) is the most underrated tool in the weaver's kit. Most people listen only to find an opening to speak. They listen for "static"—reasons to disagree or weaknesses to exploit.

An effective advocate listens to the **frequency**. Beneath the jargon of a bureaucrat or the coldness of a policy advisor, there is a human frequency: a fear of failure, a budget constraint, or a desire for legacy. When you calibrate your listening, you stop hearing an "opponent" and start hearing the words they *aren't* saying. You earn the right to speak by being the one who finally understood.

The "So What?" Filter

Run your message through the "So What?" Filter. Imagine a busy, cynical decision-maker looking at your data and asking, *"So what? Why does this matter to me, and why does it matter right now?"*

If your answer takes more than thirty seconds, or if it requires a glossary to understand, your signal is still too noisy.

- **Is it jargon-free?** If a fifth-grader can't explain your ask, you are still speaking in code.

- **Is it data-anchored?** Have you replaced the guesses with verifiable facts?

- **Is the pivot precise?** Can you redefine their objections in under two sentences?

- **Is the integrity intact?** Am I sharing this story to bridge toward a solution, or to build a monument to my own pain?

Truth is a Pin

Remember: your goal isn't to create a louder noise. Your goal is to provide the **pin**. The system is held together by bubbles of assumption and comfortable status quos. A master weaver doesn't need a sledgehammer to break those bubbles; they just need a single, calibrated point of truth.

Your lens is clean and your signal is sharp. You are accurate, honest, and ready to be heard. But even a perfect signal needs a network to carry it. It's time to move into *The Weave*, where we build the social architecture of movement-building and the generosity of shared credit.

Mastering the Weave
Section Three

The Weave is where your individual passion is multiplied. It is the shift from a solo effort to a collective mandate that is too large to ignore.

The Threads of Influence:

- **Gold (Level the Loom):** Designing for those at the furthest distance to ensure the win is universal.

- **Green (Forge Alliances):** Building alliances that are too thick to snap and too broad to ignore.

- **Gray (Lead Ethically):** Maintaining a standard of honesty that makes you a permanent fixture in the system.

- **Orange (Share the Credit):** Mastering the art of giving credit away to make the movement shine brighter.

Level the Loom
The Gold Thread

Background Music: Where The Streets Have No Name (U2)

In American healthcare, ZIP Codes can determine your destiny.[1] I chose this song because the Gold Thread focuses on "tearing down the walls" of systemic barriers. Whether it's a specialty center located a hundred miles away or a lack of translation services, these are the modern "red lines" that marginalize families. We are advocating for a system where location never determines the right to live, ensuring that every person receives the same dignity and care.

Key Idea: Equitable advocacy involves dismantling systemic barriers—race, geography, language, and socioeconomic status—to ensure equal opportunities for *every* member of the community.

Injustice anywhere is a threat to justice everywhere.

Martin Luther King, Jr.

Designing for the Median

The **Gold Thread** symbolizes justice and fairness, reflecting an unwavering commitment to ensuring that your advocacy work benefits all people equally, regardless of race, location, or socioeconomic status. Advocacy is often focused on enacting systemic change, and systems inherently carry biases based on their design.

Whether we want to believe it or not, many of the burdens people face are the result of policy choices. Decision-makers are actively choosing to make it difficult for people to access the very things they need to survive, or refusing to solve the problems at hand, all while ignoring the cries of the people they represent.

Equality assumes everyone is starting on the sidewalk. *Equity* recognizes that for many families, the starting line is the median in the middle of a highway.

Port-au-Prince, 2010

As we drove through the streets of Port-au-Prince, past the collapsed cathedrals and makeshift markets, my eyes kept drifting to the children, many of whom lived in the median of the busy road. They had nothing—no playgrounds, no schools, no toy boxes—but they were playing, as children do. I watched as they meticulously fashioned toys out of garbage, shaping discarded plastic into "cars."

Those children were the ultimate architects. They had the creativity to build, but the system around them offered no road. Equity is the infrastructure that turns a child's potential into a child's reality. Whether in Port-au-Prince or Pennsylvania, if we only build for the user with the most resources, we aren't building a solution—we're building an exclusive club.

Toy car made from garbage; Port-au-Prince, 2010

Equity isn't just about health; it's about the infrastructure of opportunity. Whether we are building a school, a transit line, or a law, we have to ask: *Who does this system assume the user is?* If we only build for the average person, we are building a blueprint that will eventually crumble under the weight of its own exclusions.

Geography of Injustice

Tori's chance at life was determined by a border.

On the same day we learned our daughter was dying, we discovered that a three-hour drive was the only difference between a death sentence and a chance at life. Had she been born in New York, she would have been screened for Krabbe disease at birth, and we could have chosen treatment. But, she was born in Pennsylvania.

Geography should never be a death sentence.

Photo by Katie Bingaman Photography

When I began my advocacy journey in Pennsylvania, I had to learn how to translate this *geography of injustice* into a language stakeholders could understand. I had to show them that for families like mine, a state line was functioning as a destiny.

We were essentially telling families that their child's right to live depended on which side of that border they were born on.

Injustice isn't always a visible villain; more often, it is a specification error—a lack of awareness encoded into law.

When we finally passed Act 133 of 2020, we didn't just add a test to a list; we tore down a border. We ensured that for the 130,000 babies born in Pennsylvania every year, a ZIP Code would no longer be a destiny.

Today, I am facing a new border—one drawn by insurance policies instead of state lines. The loom is truly never finished. Currently, my twins require hearing-related devices and services that are prohibitively expensive. While we rely on Medicaid to cover these costs due to their disability, I constantly feel the structural fragility of that protection. In many states, including Pennsylvania, private insurers are permitted to exclude hearing aids as "non-essential."

This is the embodiment of inequity: a system that requires you to be either independently wealthy or systematically impoverished just to hear. When a basic sense becomes a privilege, the architecture is fundamentally broken. A ZIP Code shouldn't be a destiny, and a policy number shouldn't be a sensory gatekeeper.

Equity isn't about providing everyone with the same thing; it's about providing the specific tools required to reach the same goal.

As a master weaver, your goal is to identify where the safety net is too narrow. Your obstacles may not be the same as those faced by others in your cause, but leveling the playing field for the most vulnerable is the gold standard of advocacy.

We don't just weave for our own families; we weave for the families we haven't met yet.

The Physical Blueprint: The Curb Cut Effect

One of the best non-health examples of equity is the "Curb Cut."[2] Activists fought for slanted curbs (ramps) on sidewalks to benefit wheelchair users (the more disadvantaged group in that system). However, once the curbs were adapted, everyone benefited—parents with strollers, travelers with suitcases, and kids on skateboards. In architectural terms, this is known as *Universal Design,*[3] but the concept spreads far beyond buildings. Advocating for the most vulnerable often leads to a better system for all.

Equity is not a special favor; it's an enhancement to the entire blueprint.

Equity is not about making everyone the same; it's about ensuring that a broken levee or a delayed diagnosis doesn't solely affect those who are already struggling to stay afloat.

The Digital Blueprint: The High-Speed Gap

Consider a town that moves its building permit process online for efficiency. If you live in a rural area without broadband, or if you're an elderly resident without a computer, you have effectively been locked out of the system. **Gold Thread** advocacy in this context would involve demanding a mobile-friendly website or establishing a physical kiosk at the library. Efficiency without equity simply results in exclusion, dressed up in a better user interface.

Some advocates worry that prioritizing equity will slow down the mission or make achieving quick wins too complex. In reality, equity serves as your most important quality-control measure. A victory that only assists the most privileged is not truly a win; it is a future failure waiting to happen. When you center the **Gold Thread**, you aren't slowing down; you are ensuring that the movement you build is strong enough to carry everyone across the finish line.

The Economic Blueprint: The Cost of Being Poor

Being poor often means facing higher costs. Think about late fees, high-interest payday loans, or the need to take three buses just to reach a grocery store that sells fresh food. When building a coalition, are you scheduling meetings at 10:00 AM on a Tuesday, a time convenient only for retirees or wealthy people? Or are you offering a bridge through childcare, evening options, or transit stipends? If participation requires time and transportation, it is not genuinely accessible to the entire public.

Equity means the system carries the burden so that families do not have to. If children in more vulnerable situations are to benefit from your advocacy, the design of the law must be robust enough to reach them where they are. We need to consider the people with the fewest resources and ask, "Does my blueprint work for them, too?"

Once you recognize the disparities, you have a responsibility to design for the most vulnerable. As Sara Groves sings, "I saw what I saw, and I can't forget it." Your advocacy is incomplete until the blueprint supports the person in need just as effectively as it supports the person in a more affluent neighborhood.

When we constructed the roof for Pastor Theodore's church in Port-au-Prince, we were not merely adding a functional building to the city; we were providing a shelter for people whom the larger system had overlooked. We were saying, "Your safety matters just as much as mine."

Equality: Providing everyone with the same resource or tool.
Equity: Providing everyone with the specific resources they need to achieve the same outcome.

The lessons learned from the **Red Thread** (Speak with Integrity) emphasize the importance of communicating our messages with clarity and purpose. However, clarity is most impactful when it aims for equitable outcomes. As you engage with the systems, remember that your ultimate goal is to ensure the change you seek benefits all families equally, especially the most vulnerable.

While equality is the baseline, equity is the ultimate aim. Your objective is to guarantee that the outcome is the same for a family on Medicaid as it is for a family with a private plane.

The *Brighter Blueprint* is not a plan for legislation; it is a plan for life. You are not powerless; you are a weaver. Every time you choose equity over ego or curiosity over contempt, you are actively changing the fabric of this nation.

> There may be times when we are powerless to prevent injustice, but there must never be a time when we fail to protest.
>
> Elie Wiesel

Why Newborn Screening is a Social Justice Issue

In the context of newborn screening, the true measure of a successful public health system is not simply the number of babies it saves, but how equally it saves them. An advocate who overlooks intersectional barriers risks celebrating a victory that leaves the most vulnerable families behind.

Social justice pertains to the fair and equitable treatment of all individuals in society. We must set aside partisanship and listen to understand the experiences of the most vulnerable and marginalized, as much of advocacy is indeed rooted in social justice.

When I first began studying Pennsylvania's newborn screening system, I quickly noticed that not all hospitals screened for the same conditions. This inconsistency creates a system in which access to timely diagnosis and treatment depends on the hospital where a baby is born, a far more concerning issue than variations based solely on the state of birth. Recognizing the need to address this issue, I initiated discussions with various stakeholders to understand the root causes of the problem and identify solutions.

This is just one example of the inequalities present in our systems, which extend beyond public health. As advocates, if we address issues only for a small group of people, we are not truly solving the problem.

Newborn screening (NBS) is one of the few medical interventions designed as a universal preventive measure. It is a promise made by the state to every resident, and it is offered to nearly every baby born in the U.S. and in many other countries. When this promise fails due to a family's location or income, the public health system is broken.

Justice demands that every aspect—from transporting the dried blood spot, lab processing, to hospital notification—occurs at the same pace in a rural hospital as it does in an urban one.

Equity goes beyond testing; it encompasses follow-up care. If a positive screening leads to a specialist whom a low-income family cannot access due to travel costs or lost wages, the system has not achieved its operational goal.

Equity is not a partisan issue; it is a matter of excellence. A system that works only for some is an inefficient machine.

> **An effective advocate doesn't just recognize obstacles; they also see the systems that created them.**

The Equitable Advocate in Action

- **Intentionally researches bias:** Actively seeks data on how race, geography, and socioeconomic status create barriers to screening, diagnosis, or treatment access within their state.

- **Partners for equity:** Goes beyond traditional patient groups to collaborate with organizations focused on justice, civil rights, and rural health.

- **Designs the dignity ask:** Ensures policy proposals include mechanisms that guarantee culturally competent care, language access, and financial support for non-medical costs.

- **Prioritizes the continuum:** Understands that success is measured by equal access to the full continuum of care for every person, especially the most vulnerable.

Equity ensures that you aren't just building for those with the loudest voices, but for those with the greatest need.

The Narrative Lens: *Hidden Figures*

The film *Hidden Figures* is one of the most powerful demonstrations of the **Gold Thread** in action. As you watch, notice how removing systemic friction is not just a moral act—it is an essential requirement for the mission's success.

The Strategic Pivot: NASA is in a high-stakes race to put a man into orbit, but the project is stalling. Katherine Johnson is a "human computer" with the exact mathematical genius they need, yet the system is designed to slow her down. Because of Jim Crow laws, she is forced to run half a mile across the campus just to find a restroom she is allowed to use.

The pivot occurs when her supervisor, Al Harrison, realizes that the system's potholes (segregation) aren't just a social issue—they are a **mission-failure issue.**

The Insight: Pay attention to the scene where Harrison takes a crowbar to the "Colored Ladies Room" sign. He famously states: **"At NASA, we all pee the same color."** The system could not afford to have its best mathematician spending forty minutes a day running to another building. The sign was a barrier to the work for which she was hired.

In advocacy, the Gold Thread represents **efficiency.** When you identify who is currently being locked out and remove those barriers, the entire mission advances more swiftly.

Equity is the key to reaching orbit.

The Gold Interlocks: Advocate for Equity

These interlocks ensure that no matter how complex the weave becomes, the safety net remains wide enough to catch the families you have yet to meet. Designing for the most vulnerable is the gold standard.

Interlock	The Asset	The Stitch
Gold + Pink Maintain Resilience	The Joy of Justice	Focus on restoration and celebration to keep the work sustainable.
Gold + White Practice Humility	Self-Aware Equity	Check your privilege daily; be a partner, not a "savior."
Gold + Silver Bridge the Divide	Bipartisan Equity	Frame fairness as a human right that transcends political sides.
Gold + Yellow Learn & Unlearn	The Inequality Audit	Use data to diagnose systemic gaps that feelings alone can't prove.
Gold + Blue Listen for the Unspoken	Lived Authority	Ensure the people most impacted by the problem are the ones designing the solution.
Gold + Gray Lead Ethically	Ethical Equity	Refuse to sacrifice long-term fairness for a temporary win.
Gold + Red Speak with Integrity	Visible Justice	Use your voice to shine a light on the families the system usually ignores.
Gold + Green Forge Alliances	Inclusive Tables	Build a coalition that actually looks like the community you serve.
Gold + Orange Share the Credit	Diverse Visibility	Share the spotlight with the quiet leaders who do the heavy lifting in the shadows.
Gold + Brown Act Strategically	Systemic Remediation	Focus on physically removing the barriers that prevent equal access.
Gold + Purple Master the Pivot	Just Adaptation	Stress-test every strategic pivot: "Does this help or hurt the most vulnerable?"

Thread Experiments: The Missing Voices

The Task: Reflect on the last stakeholder group you participated in (a meeting, an email thread, or an advisory board). Count the different types of people represented (e.g., doctors, parents, legislators, tech experts). Then, identify one group that is directly affected by the issue but was not included in that discussion. Is there a parent from a rural area present? Someone who relies on Medicaid?

The Mastery: Equity begins with asking: "Whose voice is missing from this room, and how does their absence affect the solution we are building?" You cannot address an inequity you haven't noticed.

Bonus Experiment:

Identify one non-health-focused community organization (e.g., a civil rights group, a food bank, or an organization focused on housing access) in your area. Reach out and schedule a 15-minute call to ask them: "What is the most significant barrier to health access that your clients face?" Use their response to inform your next advocacy step.

Mirror Reflection

If I were the person with the least power, the least money, and the most distance from the Capitol, would this plan still give me hope?

Gold Thread Recap

You have applied quality control to your mission, intentionally designing solutions for those furthest away to ensure no one is left behind.

The Result: Your advocacy is now anchored in equity, creating a *Universal Design* that is more resilient and just for the community.

The Next Stitch: Now that you've ensured the integrity of your weave, we move to the **Green Thread**, where we learn the power of collaboration—trading the *Solo Needle* for the *Collective Loom*.

Where you live should not decide
Whether you live or whether you die.

U2 (Crumbs From Your Table)

Forge Alliances
The Green Thread

Background Music: Safe and Sound (Capital Cities)

Most people think collaboration is simply about getting along. However, this song conveys a different message: it highlights the unstoppable momentum created when we uplift one another. When a coalition moves in sync, it becomes a tidal wave, capable of protecting the mission even in the face of political adversity.

Key Idea: Collaboration involves working with various individuals and organizations to achieve more meaningful and sustainable outcomes. In advocacy, this means forming partnerships and coalitions with different stakeholders to reach a common objective.

Alone, we can do so little; together, we can do so much.

Helen Keller

Weaving Interdependence

The **Green Thread** symbolizes the power of collaboration and partnership, enabling you to amplify your collective impact. It represents the weaving together of different threads to create something stronger than any single thread could be on its own.

This thread reflects your willingness to collaborate with a diverse range of individuals and organizations—ranging from public officials and researchers to advocacy groups. True collaboration requires humility and a focus on shared goals; it means acknowledging that you don't have all the answers and that working with others can lead to more impactful and sustainable outcomes.

My advocacy journey has been filled with a range of emotions. At first, I felt the urge to work alone because I wanted my loss to have meaning. I wanted my pain, grief, and my daughter's brief life to serve a purpose as I tried to redeem that deep loss.

However, I was mistaken in thinking that I had to work alone for it to be meaningful. In truth, her life had purpose regardless, and any actions I took in collaboration with others would have preserved that same purpose. My journey taught me that collaboration is not merely a nice-to-have; it is the very foundation of effective advocacy.

For a long time, I operated as a solo advocate. I wasn't affiliated with a nonprofit; I was "just a mom." I often feared that this would undermine my legitimacy and struggled with feelings of imposter syndrome. But I soon discovered that my most powerful resource was my personal story and my unique perspective. I learned that stakeholders were willing to support me as a mother advocating for change, and this personal approach opened doors that might have remained closed to a professional lobbyist.

In my experience, collaboration doesn't always resemble a formal team structure. Instead, my team often existed out of sight. I built it one conversation at a time—what I call linking. One conversation led to another as the links were established. My behind-the-scenes team of legislative staffers, legislators, and a former boss became my lifeline. This experience proves that personal connections, trust, and a shared commitment to a cause can be just as powerful as the resources of a formal organization.

From Solo to Symphony

Ceremonial Signing of Act 133 of 2020

The picture of our ceremonial bill signing isn't just a photo of a victory; it is a photo of a **guild.** In the photo, you see the result of *Stakeholder Theory*[1] in action: the legislator gets the "win," the lab gets a process that works, and the families get a future.

You will need a strong support system on your journey, including your spouse/significant other, family, fellow advocates, and advocacy groups. Don't be afraid to ask for advice and assistance. By sharing resources and working together, we transform a singular fight into a unified movement.

While the human instinct often leans toward independence, effective advocacy demands a different approach. Collaboration is not merely a strategic choice; it's a fundamental element for sustainable advocacy and the well-being of advocates themselves. As Adam Grant notes in *Hidden Potential*, teams are most impactful when people recognize that they need each other to succeed. "That's what enables them to bond around a common identity and stick together to achieve their collective goals."[2]

Advocacy, especially when driven by grief, can be emotionally and physically exhausting. The most crucial allies are often not found in the statehouse or boardroom; they are the people who support you on your journey. For me, that was my husband, Brennan. While I was in meetings at the Capitol, he was at home caring for our identical twin sons. He was a vital part of the team, even if few recognized this.

There is no doubt that I would not have been successful without the team I inadvertently assembled over time.

> Interdependence is the paradigm of we—we can do it; we can cooperate; we can combine our talents and abilities and create something greater together.[3]
>
> Stephen R. Covey

Why We Weave Together

As you've been exploring each thread, you might feel that you lack strength in a particular area. This is where the importance of the **Green Thread** comes into play. By building a team with diverse perspectives, skill sets, and expertise, you can collaboratively tackle any problem.

We all have unique skills to contribute. Maybe you aren't a writer or a speaker, but you love helping in practical ways. There are examples throughout history of those contributors making a big difference. One of my favorite examples is Georgia Gilmore, a cook who served the Civil Rights movement from her kitchen. She organized the *Club from Nowhere* and led fundraising efforts to support the bus boycott.[4] She eventually opened a secret restaurant in her home that served as a meeting place for leaders, including Martin Luther King, Jr.

Georgia Gilmore didn't just cook; she engineered the financial infrastructure of the Montgomery Bus Boycott. Her *Club from Nowhere* proved that a movement is only as strong as its fuel—both literal and figurative.

A support system is not solely about achieving legislative victories; it's also about the people who help you avoid burnout and keep moving forward, even by making fried chicken. We all bring different skills and viewpoints to the table, and collaboration allows a movement to grow without overwhelming the individuals behind it.

Additionally, in rare disease advocacy, many advocates are also full-time caregivers. Sharing responsibilities means that no one has to be an expert in every area, and the emotional weight is shared.

Real change occurs when solutions benefit all stakeholders. If a plan only caters to one group, the system will ultimately reject it (*Stakeholder Theory*). In *Stakeholder Theory*, a stakeholder is anyone who can affect or be affected by the mission. If the state lab is affected by your bill, but you didn't include them in the weave, they will eventually become the friction that slows you down. An effective advocate invites the friction to the table before the bill is even drafted.

What is Stakeholder Theory?

In 1984, Professor R. Edward Freeman[5] shared a simple yet powerful concept: for any mission to succeed, it must create a benefit for everyone involved, not just those at the top. As advocates, we understand that a new law won't endure if it imposes impossible tasks on a laboratory or complicates a doctor's office. To achieve lasting success, we must look at the entire picture.

You don't need everyone to be your best friend, but your solution must work within each person's reality as well. When you align everyone's needs, progress becomes inevitable.

The Power of Inclusion

Building a coalition, whether formal or informal, is a crucial step in collaborative advocacy. This process involves identifying potential partners, establishing shared goals, and navigating potential conflicts.

No one likes to feel excluded, especially in important work like rare disease advocacy. Look for individuals to bring into the conversation and experience the journey with you. By intentionally including others, you're not just increasing manpower; you're adding diverse perspectives, skills, and lived experiences. This enhances the resilience and power of your advocacy.

An inclusive approach helps you:

Enrich your perspective: Each individual affected by a rare disease has a unique journey. By including patients, caregivers, siblings, doctors, and researchers, you gain a more comprehensive understanding of the challenges and potential solutions.

Build a stronger community: A sense of belonging is vital. When people feel seen and valued, they are more willing to invest their time and energy in the cause. This transforms a small group of advocates into a large, supportive community that can amplify your message and sustain the work.

Boost credibility and reach: Inclusive advocacy demonstrates to policymakers and the public that your cause is a collective concern with broad support rather than a personal issue. Your message gains credibility when delivered by a diverse chorus of voices.

Essentials and Non-Essentials

> In essentials, unity.
> In non-essentials, liberty.
> In all things, charity.
>
> Attributed to Rupertus Meldenius

I learned this quote many years ago, and while it was originally aimed at a church whose members were in disagreement, it also applies to advocacy.

In the essentials, unity in the mission.

For our work, unity includes communication, collaboration, coordination, transparency, and inclusion. In rare disease advocacy, the essentials involve parents, families, and the patients themselves, who will likely advocate in their respective states. It also includes everyone working together in their specialties to realize the desired change.

In the non-essentials, liberty in the methods.

Flexibility is necessary to meet each state's specific needs. Some states may require more effort than others, and we must adapt while following their lead. It's important to recognize that both science and bureaucracy are constantly evolving, and we need to flow with those changes.

In any coalition, the primary essential is the mission. An example of a non-essential is the logo that is the largest on a flyer. If the flyer saves a life, the size of the logo doesn't matter. This is humility (**White Thread**) meeting collaboration (**Green Thread**).

We must remember what truly matters and put aside the rest.

In all things, charity.

In this context, we define charity as kindness, tolerance, and respect—not only toward one another but also toward stakeholders and the limitations they face. If we keep our end goal in mind, managing the non-essentials becomes much easier.

> Cooperation is the only true solution of many of our problems…realizing that individual success depends upon the success of all.
>
> Milton S. Hershey

Establish a Shared Vision and Goals

This step is crucial. A shared vision represents the future you are all working toward—for example, "a world where every child is screened and diagnosed early." This vision acts as an emotional and moral compass, keeping the coalition united. A successful collaboration is built on shared goals, not solely on shared identities. Your goals are the concrete steps that lead to achieving that vision.

Navigate Potential Conflicts

Differences in approach or opinion are inevitable. When conflicts arise, use the principles from the **Silver Thread** (Bridge the Divide), the **Blue Thread** (Listen for the Unspoken), and the **Gray Thread** (Lead Ethically). Maintain a non-adversarial stance, emphasizing shared values rather than personal disagreements.

Practice Mindful Invitation

Recognize that not every advocate can attend every meeting or event. Their inability to participate should not be seen as a rejection of the cause or of you. Continue inviting them and reassuring them that this is a safe space where it's okay to say, "I can't right now." This helps to build a community of trust and acceptance.

> We know true collaboration happened when the idea can no longer be traced to one person.
>
> Simon Sinek

Applying the Green Thread to Advocacy

In this work, it may be tempting to view the system as an obstacle. In reality, the people who run the system are your most critical allies. The most effective advocacy is achieved through collaboration with and a deep respect for those who have dedicated their careers to the field and work in the system daily. By seeking out these individuals and viewing them as partners rather than opponents, you can transform your advocacy journey. They are not the enemy; they are your collaborators.

By applying the principles of learning, listening, and communicating outlined in previous chapters, you'll create a foundation for successful collaboration. An impartial approach allows you to form partnerships with a diverse range of stakeholders, even those with whom you may disagree on other issues.

A strategic advocate understands that:

- Building a coalition involves finding allies, even if your reasons for a shared goal differ.

- No one person can fix the system. You will rely on your community not only for emotional support but also for their unique skills, resources, and connections.

- It is more effective to attend meetings with a diverse group of stakeholders than to advocate alone.

> **We weave together because the system is too vast
> for a single thread to move on its own.**

Unique Challenges of Rare Disease Advocacy

I want to acknowledge the unique challenges rare disease families face when collaborating. Many of us would never have chosen to work together if not for the shared tragedies we've experienced. This distinction is important, as it means our collaborations are often grounded in emotion rather than common professional backgrounds or political ideologies.

As a result, conflicts and frustrations may arise. We might have different opinions on the best path forward, whether it be legislative, regulatory, or prioritizing specific treatments versus broad-based research. However, if we keep in mind what we are working to accomplish and why—our loved ones—it can help us set aside grievances and concentrate on what truly matters.

The challenge of working together is also our greatest strength. Our diverse perspectives—shaped by our unique experiences with the healthcare system and our varied professional skills—enhance the resilience and power of our coalitions. By focusing on a shared, measurable goal and uniting around our common purpose, we can transform our individual tragedies into a collective force for change.

Fight for the things that you care about. But do it in a way that will lead others to join you.

Ruth Bader Ginsburg

The Narrative Lens: Ocean's Eleven

Ocean's Eleven serves as the ultimate demonstration of the **Green Thread** (Collaboration). As you watch, pay attention to the *Specialized Weave*—a strategy in which every partner stays in their technical lane, focusing on their unique skills to achieve a shared objective. While we do not endorse criminal activity, of course, this film provides an entertaining example of the **Green Thread** in action.

The Strategic Pivot: Danny Ocean aspires to execute an impossible mission. He understands that he cannot do it alone; however, he recognizes that he doesn't require eleven leaders, just eleven specialists. He recruits a pickpocket, an acrobat, an electronics expert, and a financier. The pivotal moment occurs when they stop acting as individuals and begin to function as a cohesive unit. No one attempts to perform another's role; they trust the stitch of their partners.

The Insight: Observe the final fountain scene in front of the Bellagio. There is no grand speech; the team simply stands together in silence before walking away separately. This scene illustrates the ultimate **Green Thread** victory: a group of specialists who united to solve a complex problem, executed their respective tasks in harmony, and celebrated their success without ego.

In advocacy, it's common to be a solo act, striving to manage data, lobbying, and social media all at once. This film illustrates that true power comes from specialized collaboration. When you find partners who excel in the areas you may lack, and you trust them to deliver, the impossible becomes a tangible reality.

The Green Interlocks: Build Alliances

A solo advocate is easily snapped; an alliance is an infrastructure. These interlocks turn individual effort into collective power.

Interlock	The Asset	The Stitch
Green + Pink Maintain Resilience	Community Care	Protect your people from burnout; a tired alliance is vulnerable.
Green + White Practice Humility	Relational Safety	Keep your ego small to make the alliance's "table" feel safe for everyone.
Green + Silver Bridge the Divide	The Super-Coalition	Build a nonpartisan shield that keeps the guild from fracturing during elections.
Green + Yellow Learn & Unlearn	Shared Intelligence	Treat information like a shared resource, not a secret weapon.
Green + Blue Listen for the Unspoken	The Relational Bond	Invest in "social capital" before you need to spend it on a crisis.
Green + Red Speak with Integrity	The Unified Voice	Orchestrate your messaging so the system hears a roar, not a whisper.
Green + Gold Level the Loom	Representative Strength	Design a leadership structure that actually looks like the people you represent.
Green + Gray Lead Ethically	The Integrity Pact	Vet your partners for character; one bad actor can sink the entire guild.
Green + Orange Share the Credit	Alliance Longevity	Fuel the machine by making sure no partner's hard work goes unnoticed.
Green + Brown Act Strategically	Collective Impact	Turn individual "pothole fixes" into a coordinated infrastructure project.
Green + Purple Master the Pivot	The Collective Pivot	Keep the communication lines open so the whole ship turns at the same time.

Thread Experiment: The Intro-Maker

The Task: Introduce two people in your network who do not know each other but could benefit from collaborating.

The Mastery: Creating a green impact revolves around building connections. You don't need to be at the center of every effort to strengthen the network. The strongest fabric is composed of countless interlocking stitches. Your influence grows each time you strengthen someone else's connections.

Bonus Experiment

Identify two individuals or groups you believe could be potential allies for your cause. Reach out to one of them with a simple, respectful email. The goal is not to ask for a favor right away, but to introduce yourself and your shared interests. Offer *your* assistance rather than demanding theirs.

Mirror Reflections

Reflect on a time when you tried to go it alone in an advocacy effort. What specific challenges did you encounter, and how could collaboration have made the task more effective or less burdensome?

If you were invited to join a partnership, would you feel like a valued contributor or just another ingredient in the mix?

Green Thread Recap

You have set aside the solo act to build a guild of trusted partners, recognizing that a shared mission is too thick to snap and too broad to ignore.

The Result: You have moved from a fragile, single-point-of-failure mission to a robust coalition with the power to move systemic mountains.

The Next Stitch: Because a large movement requires a strong moral center, we move to the **Gray Thread**, where we install the firewall of integrity to protect your mission from the friction of shortcuts and dishonesty.

Never doubt that a small group of thoughtful, committed citizens can change the world; indeed, it's the only thing that ever has.

Margaret Mead

Lead Ethically
The Gray Thread

Background Music: Man in the Mirror (Michael Jackson)

The path forward is rarely black-and-white. You will inevitably encounter complex situations, conflicts of interest, and moral dilemmas where the right choice may not be the easiest or most convenient one. This song serves as a powerful reminder for the Gray Thread: any systemic change begins with a commitment to personal integrity.

Key Idea: Operating ethically means choosing the right action, even when it is difficult. This involves acting with **integrity**, prioritizing **transparency**, and safeguarding **credibility**. A solid foundation of credibility relies on honesty and integrity in all advocacy efforts.

The time is always right to do what is right.

Martin Luther King, Jr.

The Work in the Dark

In Haiti, our team had a $2,000 budget to help the local community. After consulting with Pastor Theodore and local leaders, we identified their immediate needs: rice and beans for starving families, and wood and metal to build a proper roof for a church currently covered by just two tarps and some cinder blocks, especially as hurricane season approached.

However, there was a challenge. Delivering that much food in a disaster zone was dangerous. Moving supplies during the day risked robbery, as hunger drives people to desperation. Therefore, out of compassion, we decided to deliver the food under the cover of darkness. It felt like we were involved in a high-stakes heist—whispering in the shadows, moving heavy bags of rice quickly, and keeping an eye on our surroundings. It was tense and a bit scary, with no opportunities for photo ops in sight.

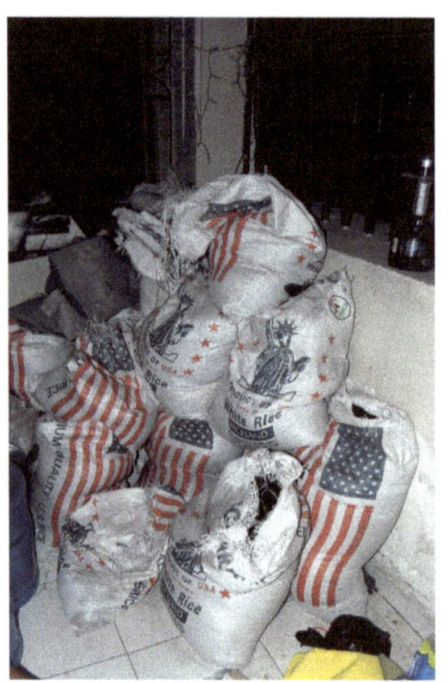

This is integrity.

In an age dominated by social media, it's easy to engage in advocacy for applause. However, effective advocates understand that the most significant work often occurs when no one is watching.

We chose not to distribute the food ourselves to avoid taking on the role of "White American Saviors," handing out bags for gratitude. Instead, we delivered the supplies to Pastor Theodore and stepped back, empowering him to serve his own community. We wanted the locals to see their leader as the provider, thereby strengthening the bond of the guild that would endure long after we returned home.

Integrity is the **Gray Thread** because it is the foundational aspect of any mission. It may not be flashy, but without it, the entire structure collapses. In your advocacy, this thread keeps you grounded, particularly when tempted to take shortcuts or exaggerate achievements for the sake of awareness. Your character must remain stronger than your platform.

To be trusted in the halls of the Capitol, you must first demonstrate your ability to deliver the "rice and beans" in the dark—and allow someone else to take the credit.

- **Check your ego at the door:** Integrity asks: Do I need to be the face of this success? If you're more concerned about who gets credit than about ensuring the roof gets built, your thread is fraying.

- **Promises kept:** We had assured Pastor Theodore that help was on the way. Integrity meant fulfilling that promise even when it was inconvenient, frightening, and went unnoticed by the rest of the world.

- **The surprise of the roof:** Later that week, we delivered roofing supplies to the church, much to their surprise. They expected more tarps; instead, we provided a roof. We didn't need to be the heroes; we just needed to be part of the supply chain.

The **Gray Thread** represents your commitment to ethical operations, serving as your unwavering moral compass that guides every action. It reminds you that true power in advocacy is not measured by the size of your victory but by the integrity with which it is achieved.

Operating in the gray— the space between perfection and compromise—requires more than just following the law; it demands making difficult decisions with transparency, honesty, and a primary focus on the long-term well-being of the community. This thread serves as your safeguard against burnout, legal missteps, and loss of trust—the most valuable asset an advocate can possess.

Do the Ends Justify the Means?

Do the ends—the vital goals you are trying to accomplish—justify the means, or do the means justify the ends? This question has fueled philosophical debates throughout history and must be settled before you begin your advocacy.

Philosophers like Machiavelli argued that the ends justify the means, suggesting that a worthy outcome excuses any tactic used to achieve it. In this view, the overall result is what matters, even if the methods used are questionable.

On the other hand, Immanuel Kant asserted that the means are as important as the ends and indeed inseparable. If the individual methods (the means) are weak or flawed, the entire outcome (the ends) will ultimately fail under the pressure of real-world implementation.

If we follow the wisdom of Frances Hutcheson, who stated that "*Wisdom denotes pursuing the best ends by the best means,*" then taking shortcuts, making aggressive demands, or exaggerating facts represents a failure in wisdom.

Gandhi warned that certain achievements accomplished through unsavory means can be destructive. This includes politics without principle and science without humanity, both of which directly apply to rare disease advocacy.

The only sustainable way is to pursue worthy ends with worthy means.

> It is not only what we do, but also what we do not do, for which we are accountable.
>
> Molière

Work Within the System

Advocacy is a long-term effort, and the best approaches are not always the quickest. In systems like newborn screening, it can be tempting to pursue a legislative mandate to bypass the slow, established process for adding conditions to the screening panel. Your bill may pass, but what if it catches public health labs off guard, leads to unfunded mandates, or forces the state to set aside a condition that is already going through the proper, evidence-based channels? Is a single victory worth damaging a system designed for scientific decision-making?

In Pennsylvania, I first addressed the obstacles that hindered progress through Act 133 of 2020. Then, I requested that the Department of Health clarify and publicly share the newly established process for adding a condition so advocates would know how to proceed. They readily agreed, and while the process is not perfect, it is now transparent.

The most effective and ethical advocates understand that our goal is not just to have our condition added, but to strengthen the process for everyone. We cannot improve the system if advocates are allowed to bypass it rather than work through it.

Sustainable change occurs from within. Instead of shouting or pushing aside established processes, we should act with integrity by asking questions to understand the reasoning behind decisions and exploring how we can help.

In advocacy, a shortcut—like a legislative mandate that circumvents the lab's capacity—is akin to creating *Systemic Debt*. You may achieve a win now, but you will pay for it later with broken trust, unfunded lab positions, and a system that is less resilient for future families. The **Gray Thread** ensures we do not sacrifice our future credibility for a quick win today.

The only way to ensure lasting success is to operate with unwavering integrity, even when it seems like a more challenging path. Integrity is not just about honesty; it often involves choosing a more complex, systemic solution over a legislative fix.

The Credibility Gap

Operating ethically is the fundamental principle that should guide every action you take. This principle is grounded in the communication theory of *Source Credibility*,[1] which suggests that a message's persuasiveness is influenced not only by its content but also by the perceived trustworthiness and expertise of the messenger. A messenger's character acts as the lens through which their data is interpreted.

When advocates behave unethically, they create a credibility gap that makes persuading decision-makers or the public nearly impossible. Ethical advocacy helps close this gap by ensuring that your actions and words consistently reinforce your trustworthiness and expertise. Your credibility is your most valuable asset.

A single lie, even if it's told for a "good cause," can undermine years of effort and erode public trust. You should never exaggerate the benefits of the solutions you advocate for. A credible advocate presents facts with integrity, acknowledging both the promises and limitations of their cause. Building relationships with decision-makers requires trust, and false information can quickly undermine that trust.

A strategic advocate understands that:

- They must never lie or mislead a legislator or official, even about what may seem like a minor detail. They recognize that losing their credibility is a setback from which they may never recover.

- They will avoid aggressive or manipulative tactics. Instead, they choose to improve the system from within by building trust rather than tearing it down with anger.

- They represent their community with integrity and professionalism, even when faced with opposition or frustration.

Adhere to the Principle of *Do No Harm*.

A compassionate advocate weighs the benefits of a proposed change against its potential for harm.

Before you take action, ask yourself:

Could my actions give other families false hope?

Could my actions create division within the community?

Could my actions cause undue stress for the professionals I am working with?

Uphold Integrity Over Allegiance

This principle is crucial when working with others. Adam Grant reminds us that *"loyalty should never come at the expense of integrity."* An effective advocate understands that a single bad thread can unravel an entire tapestry. If an ally asks you to compromise your ethical standards, you must prioritize your principles over your loyalty to an ally.

Handling Conflicts of Interest

A conflict of interest occurs when your personal or organizational interests may influence your judgment or actions in a way that conflicts with the public good. Even with the best intentions, competing interests can complicate your work.

- **Financial Conflicts:** If you receive funding from a company that could directly benefit from a policy you are advocating for, it is essential to disclose these relationships to decision-makers and the public. Transparency ensures that your message is not perceived as a sales pitch.

- **Personal Conflicts:** While sharing your personal story can be a powerful advocacy tool, it's crucial to distinguish between promoting the public good and pursuing your own interests.

- **Perceived Conflicts:** Sometimes, the mere perception of a conflict of interest can be just as harmful as an actual conflict. In the realm of policy, perception often becomes reality—stakeholders may act based on the *belief* that a conflict exists, regardless of the objective facts.

Understanding the Risk

Imagine you are a board member of an advocacy organization while also providing consulting services for a pharmaceutical company. It is crucial to keep these two roles completely separate. If you don't, there may be suspicion that your corporate connections influence your advocacy work. The best way to handle potential conflicts is to be proactive and transparent, ensuring your work is based on a solid ethical foundation.

- Always disclose potential conflicts openly and early.

- Maintain a detailed ethical policy for all staff/board members.

- Consistently prioritize the needs of the community over any personal, organizational, or financial interests.

The "Am I?" Checklist

Am I being truthful?
Have I verified all the facts and data I'm using?

Am I being respectful?
Am I treating this person as an ally or an adversary?

Am I building trust?
Will this action strengthen or weaken my relationship with them?

Am I considering the consequences?
Have I thought through the potential long-term impacts?

Am I upholding my principles?
Am I prioritizing my core values over short-term gain?

It takes less time to do a thing right
than to explain why you did it wrong.

Henry Wadsworth Longfellow

The Narrative Lens: Dave

The 1993 film *Dave* is an excellent example of the **Gray Thread** concept. As you watch, notice how simple, unwavering integrity becomes a source of power within a complex and opaque system.

The Strategic Pivot: In the film, Dave is hired to impersonate the President, but he refuses to compromise his ethics. When informed that the budget cannot support a vital social program, he doesn't just argue; he brings in a fresh perspective—his accountant—to examine the finances. He utilizes transparency and honesty as his key tools against a corrupt and manipulative Chief of Staff.

The Insight: Pay attention to the budget scene, where Dave uncovers necessary funding by cutting through the "fluff" that career experts have overlooked. This demonstrates that a Master Weaver wins by being the most honest person in the room. When your "books" are clean and your motives are transparent, you become untouchable.

Dave's power did not stem from a law degree or political background; it arose from the fact that he was the only one in the room who wasn't concealing anything. In your advocacy efforts, transparency is your greatest strategic asset.

The Gray Interlocks: Lead Ethically

In a system of shifting shadows, integrity is your only absolute currency. These interlocks ensure every strategic move is anchored in an unshakeable truth.

Interlock	The Asset	The Stitch
Gray + Pink Maintain Resilience	Ethical Self-Care	View your own wellness as a moral duty; you can't protect others if you are broken.
Gray + White Practice Humility	Teachable Integrity	Hold your values with a firm hand but your ego with a loose one.
Gray + Silver Bridge the Divide	Objective Merit	Build trust by being the most consistent, fair person in a partisan room.
Gray + Yellow Learn & Unlearn	Intellectual Honesty	Never hide a fact to help your argument; the whole truth is your best armor.
Gray + Blue Listen for the Unspoken	Confidential Trust	Treat the stories of the vulnerable as a sacred, unbreakable trust.
Gray + Red Speak with Integrity	Unassailable Advocacy	Refuse to exaggerate; a 100% honest message cannot be dismantled.
Gray + Gold Level the Loom	The Equity Mandate	Treat fairness as an ethical must, not a strategic maybe.
Gray + Green Forge Alliances	The Integrity Covenant	Let your word be the strongest currency in the alliance.
Gray + Orange Share the Credit	Honest Appreciation	Protect the value of your praise by making sure it is always earned.
Gray + Brown Act Strategically	Honest Momentum	Take the high road to the pothole; shortcuts often lead to systemic collapses later.
Gray + Purple Master the Pivot	Principled Pivot	Change your *how* as often as needed, but never your *why*.

Thread Experiments: The Conflict Check

The Task: Review your current partnerships and ask: "If this deal were on the front page of the news, would I be proud of how it was made?"

The Mastery: Your integrity is your firewall. When your records are clean, you become untouchable, and your cause becomes undeniable.

Bonus Experiment

Take a moment to complete the "Am I?" checklist for a recent advocacy-related decision you made. Reflect on your answers: Were you being truthful? Were you building trust? What could you do differently next time?

Mirror Reflections

Think of a time when you faced an ethical dilemma in your advocacy work. How did you handle it, and what did you learn?

How can you ensure your actions align with your values and principles?

Write down three ethical lines for your advocacy. What will you absolutely not do, even if it might lead to a win?

Gray Thread Recap

You have committed to a high standard of honesty and ethical conduct, refusing to trade your credibility for a win.

The Result: You have become a permanent fixture in the system—a trusted broker whose word is considered a structural fact by allies and adversaries alike.

The Next Stitch: With your integrity secured, we move to the **Orange Thread**, the final piece of **The Weave**, where we learn the strategic art of sharing the light to keep the movement bright.

Integrity is doing the right thing,
even when no one is watching.

C.S. Lewis

Silhouettes & Moments
A Poem

To be remembered
a legacy
a life well-lived
is a common and
noble desire

A human one

To know that we mattered
had an impact
are worth the space
we took up
in the collective memory

We wonder
Will we be a silhouette, a shadow,
fading over time
Or a vibrant montage persisting
in the weave we left behind?

What are we now?

In the depths of our souls
we desire to be
remembered, considered
included, loved
While we're still living

Being overlooked
forgotten, sidelined
unseen
Is there anything more painful?

How easily we forget
the way it makes others feel
when they discover they
were not remembered
didn't matter enough
weren't worth the credit

If they're not worthy
of my moments
am I worthy of their memories?
Are they worthy of mine?

I have one precious life
and so do they

Knowing this,
how much more
should we endeavor to
remember, consider

connect, include
knowing the "us" is
the only thing that lasts

After all, it is this which leads
to being remembered
when we have finally
let go of the loom

May we use our pain
from being forgotten
to do everything we can
to remember others

To pull up a chair
to share the light
and let them know:
they are remembered
they are essential
they are worth my moments

I wrote the original version of this poem a couple of years ago after a painful experience of being forgotten. I modified it to apply to advocacy and to the reality of working together to effect change.

Share the Credit
The Orange Thread

Background Music: Crowded Table (The Highwomen)

There is a specific kind of strength found in a room where everyone has a seat and every voice is valued. This song embodies the vision of an advocacy journey that isn't a lonely climb but rather a home built around a "crowded table." It reminds us that the most resilient movements are those that embrace the stories, grief, and contributions of others, intentionally pulling up more chairs.

Key Idea: Acknowledging others' contributions fosters trust and builds a stronger advocacy community. Giving credit is a strategic tool that inspires future collaborations.

It is amazing what you can accomplish
if you do not care who gets the credit.

Attributed to Harry S. Truman

The Shared Foundation

Joining the advocacy for a cause is like stepping into a novel already in progress. You may have joined the story on page 105, but you belong in these pages just as much as the pioneers who wrote the preface and the future leaders who will write the epilogue.

Effective advocates understand that they are part of a much larger narrative. The tapestry of progress is woven with the threads of countless individuals who contributed their time and passion long before you arrived. Acknowledging our place in the narrative isn't just a matter of good manners; it is a structural requirement for effective advocacy. Those who came before us hold the historical data, we bring the fresh tension, and together, we create a weave that cannot be unraveled.

To sustain a coalition, you must continuously nurture the soil in which it grows. This requires the intentional act of giving away a valuable currency: credit.

The Laborer's Anonymity

Standing inside *La Sagrada Familia* in Barcelona, you are overwhelmed by Antoni Gaudí's vision. It is a masterpiece of light, geometry, and stone. But Gaudí died in 1926, a century ago, and the project is still incomplete. He knew from the first day of construction that he would never see the final stone laid. The cathedral has been built by numerous unnamed stonecutters, architects, and donors who have dedicated their lives and resources to a vision they didn't start and might not finish. When you walk through those massive doors, you don't see a list of every person who hammered a chisel or balanced a budget. You see the vision.

This is the ultimate discipline of the **Orange Thread.**

La Sagrada Familia (Barcelona, 2024)

Gaudí provided the blueprint, but the team provided the existence. He was secure enough in his role as the architect that he didn't need to lay every brick himself. He understood that for a mission to be truly great, it must be greater than the man who imagined it.

In advocacy, true power is the ability to walk away from the paved road knowing that even if no one knows who laid the stones, no one will ever fall into that pothole again, and to let that be enough.

The Modern Cathedral

We don't put bronze plaques on every patch of asphalt or every reinforced joist in a bridge. If engineers insisted on a sign for every pothole they fixed, the road would be a cluttered mess of ego, and the focus would shift from driver safety to the vanity of the builder.

In advocacy, we are often tempted to want our name on every stone we lay. We want the credit for the bill, the quote in the paper, and the plaque on the wall. But the most durable missions—the ones that change the world for generations—are the ones where the weaver is willing to become part of the collective labor.

At first, I wanted my bill to be known as "Tori's Law," as I had seen other parents do in various states. I wanted her name to be the header of the document, a permanent testament to her existence. But that isn't how the system works in Pennsylvania.

Through this journey, I came to realize the **Orange Thread's** greatest secret: **The most durable legacy is the one that becomes invisible.** What matters is the pothole we fixed, not a sign to declare that we paved it. You can tear down a sign, but it is much harder to unpave a road that the entire community has now decided is the new standard. When you fix a pothole so well that people forget it was ever there, you have achieved the highest level of advocacy. You aren't just a character in the story anymore; you have become the foundation.

> **An effective advocate doesn't need the spotlight;**
> **they need the system to move.**

When I look at Act 133, I realize it is my *La Sagrada Familia*. It is a structure built on Tori's legacy, sustained by the unnamed lab technicians, medical professionals, and the parents I will never meet. Now, I don't see a missed opportunity for a name. I see a road that is safe for every child born in Pennsylvania. The sign doesn't matter; the structural integrity of the fix does. Like Gaudí, I had to be okay with the vision outshining the weaver.

I still mention this success when I speak, but my focus has shifted entirely to the impact, not the singular bill. When a child is identified with a rare condition through newborn screening in Pennsylvania, their parents don't say my daughter's name. They don't know who I am. And that is the highest form of self-worth: **Knowing you are so secure in your value that you don't need the system to verify it.** You have been generous enough to give the system a win that doesn't require your name to function.

Applying The Orange Thread to Advocacy

True advocacy is fundamentally a selfless act. When we commit to this work, we advocate not only for our own families but for countless others who will come after us. This larger purpose requires us to put aside ego. Striving to take all the credit, control every meeting, or do all the work alone might seem productive in the short term, but it is ultimately self-limiting. When the fight is about something bigger than ourselves, hoarding the spotlight actually dilutes our impact. It creates friction, breeds resentment, and fails to build the sustainable, wide-reaching movement necessary for lasting change.

Once you find that internal security, giving credit stops being a sacrifice and starts being a high-level tactical move. By publicly recognizing the contributions of others, you build a relational reserve of trust. It signals to stakeholders that you prioritize the mission's success over personal prestige. More importantly, it honors the *foundational weavers*—those who did the heavy lifting before you arrived—ensuring they remain allies rather than becoming obstacles.

Social Exchange Theory,[1] which was pioneered by sociologists like George Homans, teaches us that relationships are built on a series of give-and-take interactions. When you give credit, you are providing a powerful benefit—validation—which costs you zero capital. In return, you experience a multiplier effect across three areas:

Trust: Partners recognize that you won't steal their work or story.

Longevity: People stay in the fight longer when they feel their contribution is a permanent part of the pattern.

Legacy: Honoring those who came before us validates the loved ones they fought for. It ensures that when it is your turn to pass the shuttle, the next person will honor your work, too.

> According to *Social Exchange Theory*, when you provide a benefit (like public recognition) that costs you zero capital, it creates a sense of reciprocity. The receiver feels an unspoken obligation to return that value to the mission. You aren't just being nice; you are building a relational bank account you can draw from when the mission hits a pothole.

In advocacy, the spotlight is not a finite resource; it grows brighter the more people it shines on.

Remember that every fellow advocate stands beside you for their own powerful reasons. Recognizing their unique passion and purpose is key to lasting collaboration. By inviting others into the work and deliberately sharing the credit, you don't just make the journey more meaningful—you multiply the collective force applied to the system.

Never let your team, coalition, or volunteers wonder if their time is being wasted or why they are there. Keep them informed, keep them involved, and make them feel valued. If they don't feel the weight of their contribution, they will eventually disengage. A master weaver ensures that everyone at the loom understands their part in creating the pattern.

Practical Ways to Give Credit

Giving credit should be a genuine, daily practice, done with gratitude and humility rather than with a hidden agenda. While it's true that acknowledging contributions may encourage someone to do more for your cause, that shouldn't be the motivator. It should be an act of integrity (**Gray Thread**).

Here are some actionable ways to weave this into your advocacy:

Acknowledge publicly: Make it a habit to name people, organizations, and past initiatives. For example, in a presentation, you could say, "These organizations and advocates laid the groundwork for this policy, and we are now building on their hard work." On social media, be sure to tag and thank people who have helped you, even in small ways.

Refer questions: It's a sign of strength and humility, not weakness, to say, "I know someone who is an expert in this area. I'd be happy to connect you with them." This not only gives credit but also ensures the information provided is accurate and credible.

Make gratitude a habit: Reflect on how you feel when your hard work is genuinely acknowledged. Then, make a conscious effort to extend that same appreciation to others. Send a quick thank you email to a legislative aide who helped you schedule a meeting, or a text to a fellow parent who shared a resource with you. Be specific with your thank you. This simple act reinforces the value of their contributions. Don't just thank them; tell them exactly *what* they did that mattered. It proves you weren't just checking a box, but that you were truly paying attention.

> The leaders who work most effectively…never say "I."
> They think "we"; they think "team."
>
> Peter Drucker

Remember that different partners value different forms of recognition. Stakeholders, such as legislators or organizations, might prefer public appreciation in a press release, while others may appreciate a handwritten note of gratitude. For some, the most meaningful acknowledgment might be an invitation to stand at the podium with you. Thanking them in a way that matters to them is the **Orange Thread** in action.

I now recognize that grief can cloud our strategic judgment. We do not honor our loved ones by guarding a solo thread; we honor them by ensuring their thread is woven so deeply into the system that it becomes a permanent part of the fabric. True strength lies in continuing a legacy, not in competing with one.

A single thread is easy to break, but a collective tapestry is impossible to overlook. Sharing the stage doesn't diminish the legacy—it scales it.

> **Sharing the spotlight may feel like weakness,
> but, in reality, it shows confidence.**

The Mastery of the Difficult Credit

Giving credit is easy when you admire the person or the group. It feels natural to celebrate your friends. But advocacy is a complex field, and you will inevitably encounter individuals or groups with whom you've had past disagreements, competitive friction, or deep-seated resentment.

Acknowledging their contributions in those moments is not just a gesture of politeness; it is a testament to your Integrity (**Gray Thread**) and a commitment to the cause over your personal ego.

The Blurriness of Insecurity

I have found that my insecurity often drives my desire for recognition. Maybe you struggle with this, too. Insecurity is like a smudge on a lens; it clouds our vision and distorts our perception. It whispers that if our name isn't on the win, the win didn't count—or worse, *we* didn't count.

It activates our ego because the wounded part of us is trying to ensure our pain matters.

To clear the lens, we must identify the three specific ways insecurity compromises the weave:

Significance vs. Visibility: Insecurity demands the plaque because it fears the silence. It fears that if our name isn't spoken, our sacrifice wasn't seen. We confuse visibility with significance. But in engineering, the most significant parts of a building—the foundation, the rebar, the load-bearing beams—are almost always invisible. They don't need a sign to prove they are holding the weight. Are you seeking a "Thank You" to fuel the mission, or to fill a hole left by your loss?

The Need for Control: For anyone driven by high standards, credit is often a defense mechanism against the fear of being "not enough." If we own the credit, we control the narrative of our competence. Sharing it feels like giving someone else the power to mess up our "perfect" weave. Ask yourself: Is your need for credit actually a need for control? Are you afraid that if you share the spotlight, the quality of the mission will drop?

The Scarcity Mindset: Low self-esteem tells us there is only so much worth to go around. If a legislator or a partner takes a piece of the credit, we feel there is less left for our loved ones and their legacy. This is a *Scarcity Mindset*. The reality is the more people who own the win, the more people there are to defend the road when you are tired.

Think of a person or group you find difficult to work with, but who recently achieved a small win. How can you publicly (or privately) acknowledge this win without bringing up your past disagreements? It can be as simple as, *"I noticed [Stakeholder]'s work on [issue], and I appreciate the effort it took to move that forward. It's a win for the community."*

The Strategy of the Bipartisan Thank You

By concentrating on the work rather than the person, you engage in *Systemic Normalization.*[2] When you acknowledge a stakeholder for prioritizing principle over party, you demonstrate to the system that "doing the right thing" can be a successful strategy, regardless of the party affiliation. This approach heavily relies on humility (**White Thread**) to overlook past grievances and bridge building (**Silver Thread**) to recognize a universal good.

This action has a ripple effect: when a stakeholder sees a *thank you* from an advocate on the other side, it captures their attention and shows that you value results over rhetoric; they will likely see you as a partner, not an opponent; and publicly supporting a leader who crosses party lines shows that their bravery was noticed.

This approach requires you to draw on several different threads simultaneously to keep the fabric from tearing:

White Thread (Humility): Humbling your ego to speak with a rival.

Silver Thread (Bridge the Divide): You are not a partisan agent but a neutral advocate for a specific outcome, acknowledging the return on investment of integrity, regardless of party line.

Gray Thread (Integrity): You thank them because it's the truthful thing to do, not to manipulate. If someone does something commendable, a person of integrity acknowledges it.

Green Thread (Forge Alliances): Demonstrate to others in the system that you are a safe person to collaborate with, and that you value the reciprocity of the mission over turf wars.

Pink Thread (Resilience): Surprisingly, this helps alleviate burnout. When you stop viewing every opponent as a villain and start recognizing them as humans capable of pothole fixing, the emotional burden of advocacy becomes much lighter to bear.

And, of course, you are handing them the spotlight (**Orange Thread**). If you can do this, you aren't just an advocate anymore; you are a partner the system can't ignore.

The Master Weaver's Thank You Script

Keep it short, neutral, and focused purely on the act of integrity, without mentioning other disagreements.

"Representative [Name], I am writing to thank you for your recent vote on [Issue/Bill]. While we may not agree on every policy, I deeply respect your decision to prioritize principle over party in this instance. Thank you for your leadership and for doing the right thing for the families in our district."

The Generosity of Credit

In most professional spaces, we are taught to guard our wins. We worry that if we don't put our name on every press release or take the lead in every photo op, we will be overlooked, forgotten, or rendered invisible. We fear becoming a silhouette—a fading shadow of a mission that was once vibrant. But the **Orange Thread** operates on an economy of abundance rather than scarcity.

When you hoard credit, you are a solo weaver. You may create something beautiful, but it is limited by the reach of your own two hands. The moment you stop, the work stops. You become a silhouette.

When you are generous with credit, you create a vibrant montage. By inviting others to share in the victory—legislators, staffers, fellow parents, and even the unlikely allies from across the aisle—you ensure the mission is no longer tied to your individual presence. You are weave-building a community that feels a sense of ownership over the result. When you highlight the achievements of others, you are not diminishing your own; instead, you are fostering a movement that is too significant to be overlooked. By making others feel like heroes, you ensure they will remain by your side until the mission is accomplished.

To be truly effective in advocacy, you must learn to de-center your own opinion and your own ego:

Giving the win to the system: Letting a legislator believe the solution was their idea is not a loss; it is a strategic investment. If they own the win, they will defend the policy.

Redeeming the loss: We don't advocate for the spotlight. As we've noted, many of us paid dearly in personal loss. We are merely attempting to redeem that loss by ensuring the next family finds a safety net. The redemption is the reward, not the credit.

The gift of the solution: When you bring a data point or a story to a stakeholder, you are giving them a gift—the tools they need to look good while doing the right thing.

A strategic advocate understands that:

- Giving credit builds the team required to finish the race.

- Acknowledging key partners and groups by name anchors them in the mission's success.

- Unseen contributions deserve as much gratitude and recognition as those that are publicly visible.

The Narrative Lens: Toy Story

The original *Toy Story* provides a perfect illustration of the **Orange Thread**. As you watch, observe the strategic shift from individual ego to collective mission.

The Strategic Pivot: Woody is the established leader among the toys, but he feels threatened by the arrival of Buzz Lightyear. Woody tries to maintain his status and protect his territory—a mindset that ultimately leads to disaster. The pivot happens when Woody realizes that in order to get back to Andy (the mission), he must stop competing and start elevating Buzz. He acknowledges that Buzz possesses tools he does not.

The Insight: Watch for the climactic scene where Woody and Buzz use a rocket to fly. Woody isn't the hero alone; he shares the victory with Buzz, literally aligning his success with the strengths of someone else. Woody comes to understand that the "space ranger" tools he previously mocked are actually essential for their journey home.

The true enemy of your mission isn't always opposition; sometimes, it's the part of you that wants to be the *favorite toy*. If you stop competing with others' tools and start integrating and celebrating them, you'll gain the ability to fly toward your goal. In advocacy, if you claim victory alone, you risk losing an ally. However, if you share the win, you build a coalition of loyal partners for life. When you cease striving to be the *favorite toy,* you move beyond your own limitations and start benefiting from the strengths of the entire room.

The Orange Interlocks: Shine a Light on Others

These interlocks ensure your mission is built on a foundation of relational trust and a collective infrastructure. Giving credit away isn't an act of self-sacrifice; it prevents the entire mission from unraveling.

Interlock	The Asset	The Stitch
Orange + Pink Maintain Resilience	Virtuous Cycle	Find self-worth in mission progress rather than individual accolades.
Orange + White Practice Humility	Selfless Leadership	Use humility to give partners room to shine; decenter your own ego.
Orange + Silver Bridge the Divide	Cross-Aisle Validation	Prioritize the relationship over partisan criticism; acknowledge bipartisan courage.
Orange + Yellow Learn & Unlearn	Authority Network	Build collective expertise by citing the experts behind your data; move from ownership to credibility.
Orange + Blue Listen for the Unspoken	Personalized Validation	Listen well enough to know a partner's preferred style of praise and recognition.
Orange + Gray Lead Ethically	Honest Appreciation	Refuse to use hollow flattery; ensure praise is always truthful and earned.
Orange + Red Speak with Integrity	Amplified Impact	Use your microphone to highlight quiet voices and scale the message beyond yourself.
Orange + Gold Level the Loom	Equity Elevation	Proactively name invisible contributors and ensure credit reaches those in the shadows.
Orange + Green Forge Alliances	Alliance Longevity	Use consistent appreciation to prevent partner attrition and keep them in the fight.
Orange + Brown Act Strategically	Proven Value	Anchor credit in results; praise the specific work that moved the needle in the fix.
Orange + Purple Master the Pivot	Adaptive Praise	Celebrate the courage it takes to admit a mistake and pivot as much as final success.

Thread Experiments: The Unseen Thank You

The Task: Send a specific and genuine *thank you* to a behind-the-scenes person (e.g., an assistant) who helped you recently.

The Mastery: Validating the person, not just their position, builds social capital. In the system, those who feel appreciated will always go the extra mile for your mission.

Bonus Experiment

In your next meeting or email thread, attribute a good idea to someone else before they have a chance to claim it—or even if they haven't realized it was theirs. For example: "Building on what Sarah mentioned last week about lab capacity, I've drafted this proposal…" This creates a "champion." Sarah is now emotionally invested in the success of your proposal because her name is attached to its foundation.

Mirror Reflections

Am I thanking my opposition when they do the right thing, or am I so fused to my team that I am afraid to acknowledge their integrity? If my rival got all the public credit, would I still consider this a win for the mission?

Am I weaving a monument (which can be torn down) or a system (which becomes the new normal)?

Orange Thread Recap

You have mastered the art of intentionally shining the spotlight on others and ensuring the guild feels the warmth of the victory.

The Result: You have turned your success into a shared victory, building a community that feels seen, valued, and essential. And, you have built a movement that is equitable, collaborative, honest, and fueled by shared credit.

The Loom is Ready. The Strategy is Set. Now, we move to the final section: **The Momentum.** This is where the internal work and the social influence meet the hard pavement of reality. Remember, you cannot control everything. All you can do is face the world with quiet grace and hope to make a meaningful difference. Trust that being the best possible version of yourself truly matters.

Being an attentive and generous friend and citizen will prevent a thread or two of the social fabric from unraveling.[3]

Brian Doyle

Calibrating the Guild
Section Three Conclusion

This section is where the architect puts down the pen and picks up the collaborative shuttle. You have moved from the laboratory of data to the landscape of people. You have designed for the furthest distance (**Gold Thread**), built your guild of partners (**Green Thread**), installed your ethical firewall (**Gray Thread**), and mastered the art of sharing the light (**Orange Thread**).

You have built more than a campaign; you have built a social architecture. But a network is only as strong as the trust that binds it. In the heat of a campaign, when the stakes are high and partisanship tries to tear the weave apart, a poorly calibrated network will snap at the seams. To be a master weaver, you must calibrate your network to ensure it is not a solo act in disguise, but a resilient, collective force.

We often hoard power and credit because we fear being forgotten. We want our names on the bill and our faces in the photo because we want to know that we mattered. But in the architecture of impact, the desire to be a monument is actually a structural weakness.

If you are the only one who knows the strategy, the only one who talks to the press, and the only one who owns the victory, you have created a single point of failure. If you fade, the mission fades. To calibrate your legacy, you must move from the silhouette of a solo advocate to the vibrant montage of a movement.

The Economy of Abundance

The Weave thrives on a paradox: you gain more influence the more you share it. When the threads are interlocking correctly, an economy of abundance is created.

Gold (Level the Loom): Ensures the foundation is level. A network that only serves the powerful is top-heavy and will eventually collapse. Equity isn't just a goal; it's the stabilizer.

Green (Build Alliances): This is the density of your fabric. It turns a collection of individuals into a guild. By distributing the shuttle among partners, you create a mesh that the system cannot snap.

Gray (Lead Ethically): This is the firewall. One dishonest shortcut or partisan jab can compromise every node in your network. Integrity is the only currency that doesn't devalue under pressure.

Orange (Share the Credit): This is the mortar between the bricks. When you are generous with credit, you aren't losing your place in history; you are ensuring that your partners become the permanent guardians of the mission.

The Resilience Audit

The final test of your social influence is this: **If you were to step away tomorrow, would the mission continue?** If the answer is "No," your network is not calibrated; it is a monument to your own effort. A Master Weaver doesn't just build a team; they build a self-sustaining system. They use their "one wild and precious life"[1] to remember others, include them, and empower them to pick up the shuttle when the first weaver is tired.

The Final Inspection

Before moving to the *The Momentum*, run your guild through this final check:

- **Is the Orange Flowing?** Am I being generous with credit, or am I accidentally creating silhouettes of my partners?

- **Is the Green Guild Engaged?** Have I shared the *how* and the *why* with my partners so they can lead in my absence? Is this a movement of many, or a solo march?

- **Is the Gold Anchor Holding?** Does this solution still serve the family at the furthest distance, or have I compromised for a closer win?

- **Is the Gray Firewall Intact?** Am I protecting my credibility as my most valuable currency?

Your network is now calibrated for impact, not ego. You have traded the solo needle for the collective loom. You aren't just a voice anymore; you are the architect of a movement with the structural integrity to move the system.

The team is built. The social architecture is sound. But even the strongest network must know how to move through the mud of administration and the storms of unexpected change. It's time to move into *The Momentum*, where we learn to pave the road and throw the shuttle.

Building the Momentum
Section Four

Vision without execution is merely a dream, while execution without vision is just a task. Once the mindset is established, data is collected, and the team is assembled, it's time to take action. **The Momentum** emphasizes the strategic agility required to navigate challenges when the plan encounters obstacles. Strategic action is the art of pulling the right thread at the right moment to bring the vision to life.

The Two Pillars of Strategic Execution:

- **Act Strategically (Brown):** The technical efforts necessary to address issues and remove barriers.

- **Master the Pivot (Purple):** The capability to adapt the strategy while remaining focused on the core mission.

Act Strategically
The Brown Thread

Background Music: That's The Way It Is (Celine Dion)

The world doesn't always operate on our timeline. In advocacy, "That's the way it is" isn't a surrender; it's the starting point. This phrase acknowledges the challenges and the slow-moving currents of government. This thread represents the relentless hope needed to work within that reality until victory is achieved.

Key Idea: While other threads address feelings and connections, the **Brown Thread** focuses on the mechanics of advocacy. It serves as the engine, emphasizing the disciplined effort required to transform abstract ideas into concrete, systemic progress.

We remember what you did
long after we forget what you said.

Seth Godin

Moving from Principle to Performance

The **Brown Thread** symbolizes the practical and grounded act of taking action. It involves the hard work of turning ideas and plans into tangible results and the disciplined drive to make that progress impactful. In the early days of my advocacy, I learned that while the ultimate goal may be a skyscraper, the real work lies in fixing the potholes.

Taking action is essential in advocacy, but it doesn't always manifest as a heroic rush. It often involves the disciplined choice to tackle manageable problems that, over time, lead to significant and lasting change. This requires persistence, not pushiness.

Persistence: The Rhythmic Shuttle

Persistence is the rhythmic, manual labor of fixing potholes, staying in the room until the job is done. An architect of change understands that the system is often slow, not necessarily hostile. The goal is to be helpful while maintaining the mission's momentum.

The Persistence Ask: *"I noticed we haven't received the updated draft of the regulation yet. How can I help move this forward, or is there a specific hurdle our team can help address?"*

Pushiness: The Structural Snag

Pushiness happens when an advocate lacks humility (**White Thread**) or neutrality (**Silver Thread**). It treats the person across the table as an obstacle rather than a potential partner, increasing the risk of getting yourself kicked out or ignored before the job even begins.

The Pushy Ask: *"I've emailed you three times today. This is unacceptable. Why haven't you responded yet? I'm calling your supervisor."*

Persistence means consistently attending key advisory board meetings, sending weekly email updates, or following up on a legislative request until you receive a response. Strategic action is targeted, well-planned, and aligned with a specific, solvable problem. Sometimes, the action necessary is the last thing you might expect.

The Avocado Pivot

In the streets of Chimaltenango, Guatemala, I learned a lesson that transformed my understanding of impactful action. While walking through a local neighborhood, we saw a woman selling avocados. They were beautiful—perfectly ripe and vibrant green. Three of us approached her and, after a quick mental currency conversion, realized that for just twenty American dollars, we could buy her entire stock.

Avocados in Chimaltenango; 2014

Our intention was not to perform an act of charity; we acted out of excitement, wanting the avocados for our group dinner that evening. What we didn't anticipate was the humility we would feel in response to her reaction.

In that moment, we unknowingly filled a pothole for her that we didn't even know existed. She was overwhelmed by our purchase and shared with us that we had given her the most valuable resource: time. We gave her back her day. She could go home to her family, rest, or move on to the next task, relieved of the burden of sitting on a street corner.

This is the **Brown Thread** in real, everyday life.

The Power of the Small Fix

Meaningful and lasting change often comes from addressing small, manageable issues—like fixing potholes—within the existing system, rather than solely aiming for grand legislative victories, represented by skyscrapers. While the appeal of a skyscraper, such as a new, sweeping law, can be strong, an exclusive focus on monumental goals may lead to paralysis by scale and ultimately result in burnout.

The pothole approach is best understood through *Incrementalism*, a social change theory suggesting that the most stable progress is achieved through a series of small, continuous adjustments rather than giant, disruptive leaps.[1] In advocacy, *Incrementalism* is a powerful strategy; it enables you to avoid the all-or-nothing battles that often lead to gridlock.

Potholes: These are the small, frustrating, yet highly actionable issues—such as a broken form, an outdated regulation, or a missing checkbox—that, when fixed, create a smoother, more resilient system.

Skyscrapers: These represent grand, sweeping changes that are often difficult and time-consuming to achieve. They are the "ribbon-cutting" moments that make headlines but can be fragile.

The Durability of the Road

A skyscraper (like a new law) can easily be dismantled by a new administration or cut from the budget. However, when you fix a pothole, such as clarifying regulations or streamlining administrative processes, it becomes part of the system itself. It is much harder for stakeholders to un-fix a process that has evolved into a new best practice. These small wins are often stealth successes; they integrate into the system so thoroughly that they eventually become invisible.

Fixing these potholes isn't a lesser form of advocacy; in many cases, it is more sustainable and impactful. These victories are built on principles of humility, collaboration, and ethical action.

Incrementalism: The Power of the Small Wins

Many problems can be addressed simply by you taking the initiative. Identify three **Incremental Wins** that you can achieve this week. These tasks should:

- **Require no one's permission.**

- **Take less than 30 minutes.**

- **Slightly improve the system (or someone's day).**

In any moment of decision, the best thing you can do is the right thing, the next best thing is the wrong thing, and the worst thing you can do is nothing.

Theodore Roosevelt

The Avocado Principle

Remember, shoveling the sidewalk doesn't change the city's laws, but it does improve the walking experience for those using it. When you find yourself stuck in a challenging situation (skyscraper) that feels unproductive, look for a simple problem to solve (pothole). Taking small actions builds momentum. By the time you return to the bigger issue (skyscraper), you'll have gathered momentum from the little victories (the paved road) behind you.

Action is a Scale, Not a Destination

In the world of advocacy, we often feel paralyzed by skyscraper thinking, believing that if we aren't passing a federal mandate or raising a million dollars, we aren't making progress. We can become so focused on the distant goals that we trip over the immediate challenges right in front of us. But the **Brown Thread** reminds us that action exists on a scale. Sometimes, action involves high-level plans such as funding roofing supplies for a church in Haiti that currently only has tarps. Other times, it may be as simple as buying avocados for a meal or shoveling your neighbor's sidewalk. **Both types of actions are essential: one addresses systemic issues while the other improves daily life.**

The master weaver understands that you cannot build a skyscraper until you've mastered the art of paving the path ahead.

We left that market in Chimaltenango changed. We realized that our resources—our money, our time, our voices—are tools meant to be used, not trophies to be kept.

Don't just wait for the big win; look for the small opportunities. Buy the avocados. Fill the pothole. Buy someone back their day. Sometimes, when we feel overwhelmed, we need to take the next right step, both for ourselves and for our cause.

Avocado Moments

Identify the Immediate Burden: What is the one small thing stalling a family's progress today? Is it a confusing form? A missing signature? A bag of crackers?

Scale Your Solution to the Need: Don't attempt to build a bridge when all someone needs is a shovel. Sometimes, a single phone call to a staff member is more impactful than a prolonged awareness campaign.

The Humble Impact: Never underestimate the ripple effect of addressing one small problem. By relieving one person's burden, you allow them the capacity to engage and contribute further.

The Scientific Method of Advocacy (PDSA)

The most effective advocates approach their work not as passive waiting, but as a series of active, measured experiments. The *Scientific Method of Advocacy* is a strategic framework that ensures every action leads to learning, refinement, and eventual success.

The *Scientific Method* is a systematic process for answering questions and minimizing bias by testing a hypothesis (idea) against observable, measurable reality. Although it's essential in science, it is also a crucial aspect of an effective advocate's mindset. Like me, it may have been a while since you took a science class, so let's review the steps together:

- **Observation:** Define a problem based on what you see.

- **Hypothesis:** Propose a testable solution or explanation.

- **Experimentation (Testing):** Execute a controlled action.

- **Analysis:** Measure the results against the initial hypothesis.

- **Conclusion:** Refine the hypothesis based on the data.

The *Scientific Method* is directly related to what is known as the PDSA Cycle,[2] which is foundational for quality improvement.[3] I don't want this section to feel like a textbook, so I will summarize the key elements:

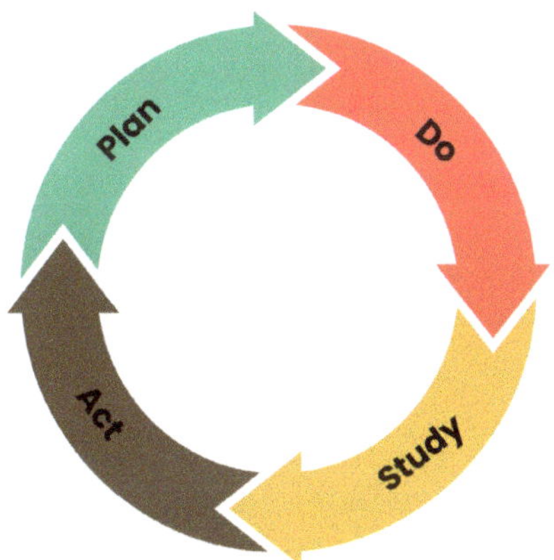

P – PLAN: Identify the Specific Pothole

Before launching a massive campaign, define the smallest, most focused action you can take to address a specific issue. This stage demands precision and humility and requires the use of *S.M.A.R.T. Goals*, a method developed by George T. Doran.[4] What specific, small action will you take to achieve your goal?

S.M.A.R.T. Goals Checklist

Specific: Clearly define the what, why, and how of your action.

Measurable: Include a metric to analyze success or failure.

Achievable: The goal must be realistic given your current resources.

Relevant: The action must align with your larger mission (the *why*).

Time-Bound: A goal must have a deadline to create urgency.

D – DO: Implement a small, controlled change

Implement the plan exactly as defined, within the smallest possible scope. This keeps risk low and enables quick learning and strategic, measured execution.

- **Pilot the Action:** Test it on a small, representative sample (e.g., five key staffers), not across the entire system.

- **Gather Data:** Meticulously record the results against your chosen metric. Track not just what happened, but when and how.

S – STUDY: Analyze the Results

This is the most critical and often overlooked phase. You must objectively measure your action against your prediction. This is where learning (**Yellow Thread**) and listening (**Blue Thread**) come into play.

- **Compare:** Did your predicted outcome match the actual outcome?

- **Analyze the Why:** If it worked, what was the driver of success? If it failed, what was the barrier?

- **Crucial Step:** Never blame the system or the people. **Blame the hypothesis.** You are testing your plan, not your integrity. A failed test is not a defeat; it is new, valuable data.

A – ACT: Adopt the change or pivot to a new plan

Based on what you learned, you decide the next step. This is the **Purple Thread (Flexibility)**—the ability to pivot based on evidence.

- **If the Test Succeeded (Standardize):** Adopt the successful method and implement it on a larger scale. This becomes your new best practice.

- **If the Test Failed (Refine):** Adjust your original plan (Pothole, Goal, Hypothesis) and restart the cycle. The failed experiment gives you better information for the next iteration.

The **PDSA Cycle** is an essential approach for transforming actions into measurable insights and setbacks into strategic opportunities. It ensures that your efforts are **grounded in evidence** and aligned with the most effective path to change. By applying this cycle, you move from guessing whether your advocacy is effective to *demonstrating* it.

What does this look like in advocacy?

Identify a specific *pothole* in your area of advocacy and break it down into actionable steps:

The Problem: What part of the process feels slow, broken, or unfair?

The Root Cause (Pothole): What is the specific cause of this?

The Authority (The Paving Crew): Who has the actual power to change this? *Sometimes it is you (avocados), sometimes it's the government.*

Once you've identified the pothole and the authority, don't try to fix it all at once. Use the PDSA (Plan-Do-Study-Act) mindset to break it down.

Often, advocates worry that focusing on small, "pothole-sized" victories makes them seem small-minded or causes them to lose sight of the big picture. However, consistent action is the only way to build the credibility required to tackle larger objectives.

During Tori's last year of life, most of my advocacy occurred from my recliner while caring for her. My first act of external advocacy was a single conversation at a Pennsylvania Newborn Screening Advisory Board meeting. That conversation sparked more discussions and gradually developed into a collective movement.

What *Schoolhouse Rock* and my political science degree didn't teach me was that advocacy is a marathon, not a sprint. I never imagined it would take three legislative attempts and 2,292 days from Tori's diagnosis until the law was enacted. However, I also didn't expect to learn how to shift from fighting the system to building a blueprint to strengthen it.

There was a great deal of trial and error, and I learned that the changes with the greatest impact are often the ones that go unseen. When you master the **Brown Thread**, you're not settling for less; you are demonstrating to the system that you are a finisher.

Small fixes aren't a distraction from the revolution—they are the bricks that build it.

An ounce of action is worth a ton of theory.
Ralph Waldo Emerson

The Narrative Lens: Finding Nemo

Finding Nemo serves as an excellent case study for understanding the concept of the **Brown Thread**. As you watch the film, pay attention to the discipline required to navigate a vast, overwhelming system through incremental and purposeful steps.

The Strategic Pivot: Marlin's goal is to achieve a *skyscraper*: rescuing his son from a dentist's office in a distant city. For a single fish, the ocean is an unpredictable environment that cannot be conquered by speed alone. Marlin's success stems from his willingness to follow a specific plan. He must memorize the exact address, navigate the "EAC" (the existing infrastructure of the current), and solve a series of immediate *potholes* just to stay in the game.

The Insight: Observe the "Tank Gang" sequence, where the fish attempt to escape from the dentist's office. They don't just "wish" for freedom; they execute a literal **PDSA Cycle**: They hypothesize that jamming the filter with a pebble will force a manual cleaning (**Plan**); they physically place the pebble—the smallest possible action toward the goal (**Do**); they observe the result. Does the gear stop? Is the water getting dirty? (**Study**). When the first attempt fails, they don't abandon the mission; they refine the plan and try again with a different mechanical approach (**Act**).

In advocacy, *Sydney* represents the policy being implemented. This film illustrates that you don't reach your destination by merely being the biggest fish in the room; you achieve it by knowing the address of those in power, riding the currents of the existing system, and having the discipline to fix the filter one pebble at a time.

The Brown Interlocks: Grounded Action

Strategy without action is a ghost; action without strategy is a mess. These interlocks ensure your pothole fixes are precisely placed to hold the weight of broader policy change.

Interlock	The Asset	The Stitch
Brown + Pink Maintain Resilience	Resilient Momentum	Pace your physical labor to avoid burnout; choose the steady rhythm of a marathon over a sprint.
Brown + White Practice Humility	Grounded Humility	Let the quality of the work speak louder than the person doing it.
Brown + Silver Bridge the Divide	Nonpartisan Infrastructure	Design solutions that ensure the pothole fix outlasts the current political season.
Brown + Yellow Learn & Unlearn	Evidence-Based Execution	Don't move a shovel until you've mapped the terrain.
Brown + Blue Listen for the Unspoken	Responsive Operations	Ensure the work being done is the work actually needed.
Brown + Gray Lead Ethically	Articulated Action	Translate plans into clear, actionable steps that anyone can follow.
Brown + Red Speak with Integrity	Integrity in the Action	Use storytelling to show how small, operational changes create massive systemic integrity.
Brown + Gold Level the Loom	Collaborative Logistics	Distribute the workload across the guild; create a shared, sustainable community effort.
Brown + Green Forge Alliances	Ethical Implementation	Ensure the way you achieve the goal is as clean as the goal itself.
Brown + Orange Share the Credit	Verified Progress	Document the small wins along the way to keep the team's morale high during the grind.
Brown + Purple Master the Pivot	Operational Agility	Be ready to change your physical approach the moment the blueprint requires a pivot.

Thread Experiment: The Desktop PDSA

The Task: Set a 60-second timer. Your mission is to build the tallest tower possible using exactly ten random items from your desk, such as a stapler, a coffee mug, or a phone. Approach this as a high-stakes puzzle. If your tower collapses, don't just become frustrated—**analyze** what went wrong (for example, was the base too narrow?). **Develop** a new strategy, **conduct** a second test, and **take** action to refine your best approach.

The Mastery: Advocacy isn't about luck; it's about maintaining a disciplined cycle of solving one puzzle at a time until your tower stands.

Bonus Experiment

Review your advocacy to-do list for the coming week. Identify which tasks are busywork (actions that feel productive but don't make a significant impact) and which are purposeful actions (targeted at a specific, solvable issue). How can you exchange one hour of busywork for one hour of engaging in the PDSA cycle?

Mirror Reflection

Reflect on an advocacy effort that didn't succeed. Rather than blaming those involved, identify a specific flaw in your original hypothesis that the data revealed to be incorrect. What valuable new insight did this failure provide for your next approach?

Brown Thread Recap

You have embraced strategic action, focusing your energy on the small, administrative potholes that determine whether a mission actually reaches the people it serves.

The Result: You have built a sustainable foundation for your cause, ensuring that your skyscraper victories are supported by a road that doesn't crumble.

The Next Stitch: Because the road rarely stays flat, we move to the **Purple Thread**, where we learn the art of strategic fluidity—the ability to pivot your tactics without losing sight of your mission.

If you see something that is not right, not fair, not just, you have to speak up. You have to say something; you have to do something.

John Lewis

Master the Pivot
The Purple Thread

Background Music: I'm Still Standing (Elton John)

In advocacy, encountering failure is common, and setbacks are often unavoidable. The Purple Thread symbolizes our key strategic shift. It represents the voice of a survivor who recovers, overcomes obstacles, and finds a stronger way to stand.

Key Idea: Flexibility is a strategic pivot grounded in evidence, prioritizing the ultimate goal over the initial plan. It involves the disciplined decision to abandon or modify an ineffective strategy when data or stakeholder feedback suggest a more efficient route.

Let no one think that flexibility and a predisposition to compromise is a sign of weakness or a sell-out.

Paul Kagame

Fluid and Flexible

When I arrived in Port-au-Prince shortly after the 2010 earthquake, the devastation was beyond description. Buildings weren't just damaged; they were reduced to gray dust that blanketed everything. The infrastructure we rely on in the West—paved roads, clear schedules, and functioning power—didn't exist.

During our orientation, a seasoned disaster relief leader shared a piece of advice that transformed my perspective on advocacy: **"Flexible things can eventually reach their limit and snap. Fluidity moves around the obstacle and keeps going."**

At that time, I was someone who depended on spreadsheets and planners. I liked to know exactly where the "piles of rubble" were so I could plan my route around them. But in a broken system, the rubble shifts. The obstacles change.

The Snap Point vs. The Flow

In advocacy, we often take pride in being flexible. We adjust our talking points for different legislators or reschedule meetings. However, flexibility still entails a certain amount of tension. Bending a rigid structure means that if the system's pressure becomes too high, we will eventually hit our breaking point.

Fluidity, however, is different. It enables us to flow into the cracks of a broken system. When a bill gets stalled in committee, a flexible advocate might feel frustrated that their plan is being bent. In contrast, a fluid advocate simply looks for the next opportunity—a different staffer, a new administrative rule, or another pothole to fill—and continues moving toward their goal. They strategically pivot.

The Fluidity Audit

Am I attached to the plan or the outcome? Flexible people are attached to the plan. Fluid people are obsessed with the outcome.

Where is the crack? If the main road is blocked by rubble, don't stand there trying to move the rubble out of the way. Look for the side street.

Am I holding my breath? Flexibility feels like holding your breath while you bend. Fluidity feels like breathing through the movement.

Applying the Purple Thread to Advocacy

The **Purple Thread** is the essential final stage of the *Scientific Method of Advocacy*—it represents the STUDY and ACT phases of the PDSA cycle. Flexibility is the ability to adapt your strategy, bend without breaking, and pivot when objective data (**Yellow Thread**) demands a change in direction. It is the resilience (**Pink Thread**) that prevents burnout and keeps your cause moving forward.

An effective advocate understands the need to wait for the right moment to act, ensuring that their efforts contribute to solutions rather than unintentionally harming the system they aim to improve. This strategic patience is a form of flexibility, and it is a *strength*, not a weakness. It entails taking a moment to evaluate the situation because rushing into action can often cause more harm than good.

Learning about the systems, stakeholders, and potential solutions takes time, and the path you start on may not necessarily lead to success. Practicing patience and flexibility helps your strategy adapt to unexpected challenges.

Advocacy often requires strategic flexibility on three major fronts, forcing you to prioritize the outcome over the pathway:

- **Flexibility on the Mechanism:** Whatever your ultimate goal is, the mechanism can be legislative (a new law) or regulatory (an administrative rule change). The regulatory approach can be just as effective, if not more so, than the legislative approach.

- **Flexibility on the Timeline:** Policy change takes time, which can lead to burnout among advocates. Being flexible means adjusting your understanding of success to accommodate a multi-year timeline. For instance, if a listening session (**Blue Thread**) reveals a competing priority that will cause a delay, act by immediately shifting your goal to secure a promise for priority scheduling in the next session, using the intervening time to address administrative challenges.

- **Flexibility on the Solution:** Sometimes, the best way to counter scientific or financial concerns is to agree to start with a smaller, controlled test. For example, if the Newborn Screening Advisory Board is worried about the false positive rate, you could propose a pilot study in one county or hospital for a defined period, with clear, measurable metrics. This strategic compromise reduces risk and makes full adoption easier in the future.

Separate the Person from the Plan

The greatest enemy of flexibility is emotional attachment to a plan. When you are deeply invested in seeing your specific bill language passed, you might overlook data indicating that a regulatory solution (a faster, more permanent fix) is more effective.

The Emotional Trap: We often become emotionally attached to the *how* (the specific bill number, event, or talking points) rather than focusing on the *what* (the ultimate outcome: babies being screened) or the *why*.

The Pivot Mindset: Treat your plan like a hypothesis in the scientific method: it should be seen as disposable. When the STUDY phase of the PDSA (Plan-Do-Study-Act) cycle reveals a failure, the ACT phase requires you to discard the failed plan and explore a new hypothesis.

Strategic Flexibility is Not an Ethical Shortcut

There is a clear distinction between strategic flexibility (changing how we achieve our goals) and taking ethical shortcuts (abandoning the reasons behind our actions). Strategic flexibility involves adjusting our tactics while maintaining our moral principles. As the **Gray Thread** emphasizes, it is crucial to conduct ourselves with integrity in everything we do.

How to tell the difference:

Transparency: Can I explain to my community how we achieved this success without feeling ashamed?

Equity: Does this new approach leave the most vulnerable families behind just for quicker results?

Sustainability: Does this shortcut jeopardize the efforts of future advocates?

A strategic advocate understands that a *Side Door* is still a door—it is built on the same foundation of truth and service as the *Front Door*. It simply offers a different way to enter the building.

It's important to recognize that compromise isn't a negative term in this context; we can also think of it as a pivot. For instance, during our final legislative attempt, an influential stakeholder opposed our modified bill language. This prompted us to meet with them and others to listen to their concerns. The stakeholder proposed an alternative method for funding the newborn screening program. Initially, I was reluctant to agree. I believed our plan was solid and would address the existing issues, and I felt attached to it.

However, as we discussed the options, the legislative director and I realized that the stakeholder's proposal could lead to greater program growth in the future. We decided to compromise with them, ultimately strengthening our law.

If we refuse to consider a compromise, we risk being ineffective.

The Sunk Cost Fallacy

In advocacy and in life, we often fall into the trap of the *Sunk Cost Fallacy*[1]—the belief that we must continue a failing strategy simply because we've already invested time, money, or emotion into it.[2]

You might think, "We've been pushing this specific bill for three sessions. We can't change the language now!" or "I've spent two years building this specific coalition. I can't walk away even though they aren't aligned with the mission anymore."

The reality is that an engineer doesn't keep building a bridge on a cracked foundation just because they already poured the concrete. They stop, demo the work, and start over. In advocacy, your marathon only works if you are running in the right direction. If you realize the road is a dead end, the most effective move you can make is to unravel the row.

How to Identify the Sunk Cost Snag:

Ask yourself: "If I were starting this mission today, knowing what I know now, would I choose this specific path, partner, or policy?" If the answer is "No," you aren't quitting—you are pivoting. You are protecting the future of the mission from the mistakes of the past.

The **Purple Thread** is about strategic agility. The *Sunk Cost Fallacy* prevents agility. Give yourself permission to let go of what isn't working so you can save the mission.

Is it time to unravel?

The "Clean Loom" Question: If I were starting this mission today, knowing what I know now, would I choose this specific partner, policy, or tactic? (Yes/No)

The Resource Drain: Is the energy required to save this failing strategy stealing resources from a pothole I could actually fix? (Yes/No)

The Integrity Check: Am I staying on this path because it works, or because I'm afraid of how it would look if I stopped? (Works/Fear)

The Master Weaver's Mantra: *I am not a quitter; I am an optimizer. My hands are too busy weaving the future to cling to a strategy that belongs in the past.*

It is not the strongest of the species that survives, nor the most intelligent that survives. It is the one that is the most adaptable to change.

Charles Darwin

The Advocate's A.D.A.P.T. Framework

A — Assess the New Information: Acknowledge what you don't know and become a student to learn more.

D — Define the Impact: Determine whether this change affects the outcome or just the perception. Have the courage to redefine your objectives, as new scientific discoveries or shifts in legislators' priorities may require you to change your focus. Ask yourself, "Does this pivot change the outcome or just the optics?" If the outcome stays the same, then the pivot is a success.

A — Adjust Your Strategy: Be willing to abandon familiar methods in favor of effective ones. Have the courage to change your strategy and try something new. This step involves reevaluating your game plan without losing sight of your ultimate goal.

P — Pivot with Purpose: Clearly communicate the rationale behind your strategic shift to your team. Have the courage to explain why you are changing direction, ensuring your team remains aligned and trusts your decisions.

T — Take Action (and Rest): Recognize when the best pivot is to take a tactical pause. Have the courage to say "no" when your energy is low, understanding that self-care is an act of resilience, not weakness.

When the "Front Door" Slams, A.D.A.P.T.:

- **Assess:** Determine if the "No" is based on financial, scientific, or political reasons (*The Pattern*).

- **Define:** Consider whether changing the approach (the *how*) affects the underlying reasons (the *why*).

- **Adjust:** Shift your focus from solving large, complex issues (skyscrapers) to addressing smaller, manageable ones (potholes) (**Brown**).

- **Pivot:** Inform your team that you aren't stopping, just pivoting.

- **Take Action/Rest:** Sometimes, the best course of action is to wait (**Pink**).

The **Purple Thread** ensures that you are always making progress, even if it isn't in the direction you initially intended. While the goal remains fixed, the path to achieving it must remain adaptable.

Advocates often fear that changing their minds or admitting a tactical defeat might portray them as inconsistent or weak, but in truth, strategic flexibility is the hallmark of a master architect. Rigidity can lead to the collapse of movements, while flexibility allows them to endure. When you master the pivot, you're not being indecisive; you're responding effectively to reality.

The Narrative Lens: Apollo 13

Apollo 13 is the ultimate demonstration of the **Purple Thread**. As you watch the film, take note of how the team reinvents their approach the moment their original plan falls apart.

The Strategic Pivot: Following an explosion on the way to the moon, the mission shifts instantly from "landing" to "surviving." The original flight plan becomes obsolete. The engineers on the ground must pivot into the **Purple** mindset. They face a critical issue: the crew's carbon dioxide filters are failing. They need to fit a square filter into a round hole, using only the "junk" currently available on the spacecraft.

The Insight: Pay attention to the "Square Peg in a Round Hole" scene where the flight director dumps a box of parts onto a table, instructing the team to devise a fitting solution. This exemplifies strategic flexibility in its purest form. The ultimate goal—getting the crew home—remains unchanged, but the pathway to achieve it is reinvented in real-time, informed by existing constraints.

In the **Purple Thread** approach, you don't wait for additional resources—be it more money, more staff, or more recognition. Instead, you utilize the resources you already possess—a contact in a lab, a sympathetic legislative aide, or a singular success story—and build an alternative solution using those exact elements. When one door closes, a master weaver doesn't give up; they assess the parts available and create a new way forward.

The Purple Interlocks: Maintaining Flexibility

Rigid things snap under pressure; fluid things find a way. These interlocks provide the structural support to pivot without losing your path. A bent thread is still part of the weave; a snapped one is lost forever.

Interlock	The Asset	The Stitch
Purple + Pink Maintain Resilience	Adaptive Peace	Keep your team calm by staying in solution mode when the map changes.
Purple + White Practice Humility	Fluid Humility	If Plan A is failing, be the first to suggest Plan B.
Purple + Silver Bridge the Divide	Political Maneuverability	Reframe the *why* to stay relevant regardless of who wins the election.
Purple + Yellow Learn & Unlearn	Intelligent Agility	Let new data be the commander that dictates your next strategic move.
Purple + Blue Listen for the Unspoken	Anticipatory Listening	Read the room's energy to pivot before the door is slammed shut.
Purple + Red Speak with Integrity	Narrative Agility	Treat your pitch like a conversation; if they aren't nodding, change the song.
Purple + Gold Level the Loom	Just Adaptation	Never trade the well-being of the vulnerable for a faster path.
Purple + Green Forge Alliances	The Collective Turn	Turn the ship together; transparency is the fuel for a coalition's pivot.
Purple + Orange Share the Credit	Adaptive Praise	Celebrate the bravery it takes to admit a mistake and try something new.
Purple + Gray Lead Ethically	Principled Pivot	Change the road, but never change the North Star.
Purple + Brown Act Strategically	Responsive Action	Move resources to where the road is actually being built.

Thread Experiments: Pivot Practice

The Task: Reflect on a minor plan that went wrong today, such as a canceled meeting or unexpected rain, and find an alternative that still achieves the original goal.

The Mastery: A strategic advocate never feels blocked for long. When one path closes, you possess the strategic resilience to assess the situation and build a better way forward.

Bonus Experiment

Your goal is to keep your smartphone upright at a 45-degree angle for a video call. You are forbidden from using a phone stand, a tripod, or leaning it against a wall/laptop. You have 60 seconds to "MacGyver" a stand using only three items found in your immediate workspace (e.g., a coffee mug, a binder clip, a stapler, a pair of sunglasses, or tape). Assemble your creative solution and ensure the phone stays upright for ten seconds. While the outcome (the video call) remains unchanged, the method has altered. If you can stop focusing on the absence of the tripod and start utilizing a creative solution, you demonstrate mastery of the **Purple Thread**.

Mirror Reflection

Identify one element of your current goal that you could strategically compromise on without sacrificing the fundamental well-being of the people you serve. Why would this compromise be a strategic ACT phase move?

Purple Thread Recap

You have mastered adaptive action, choosing to be fluid and flexible—refusing to let a changing map or a closed door stop the flow of your mission.

The Result: You are now unstoppable, possessing the agility to navigate around obstacles and the humility to change your *how* to protect your *why*.

The Next Stitch: Your loom is full. Every thread is now interlocked into a single, cohesive fabric. We move now to the **Final Knot**, where we learn the science of succession—ensuring the tapestry continues to grow long after the first weaver has moved on.

We cannot direct the wind, but we can adjust the sails.

Dolly Parton

Calibrating the Momentum

Section Four Conclusion

You have reached the end of the technical labor. You have paved the road through the administrative grind (**Brown Thread**) and mastered the art of the strategic pivot (**Purple Thread**). You have successfully transitioned from a person with a story to an architect with a blueprint in motion.

The Momentum is now established. The shuttle is moving, the pattern is visible, and the system is beginning to respond to your rhythm. But the final test of an engineer isn't just that the machine runs—it's that it stays running when the engineer walks away.

Before we tie the final knot, we must ensure the engine is tuned for the long haul. We aren't just looking for a win; we are looking for a **standard.**

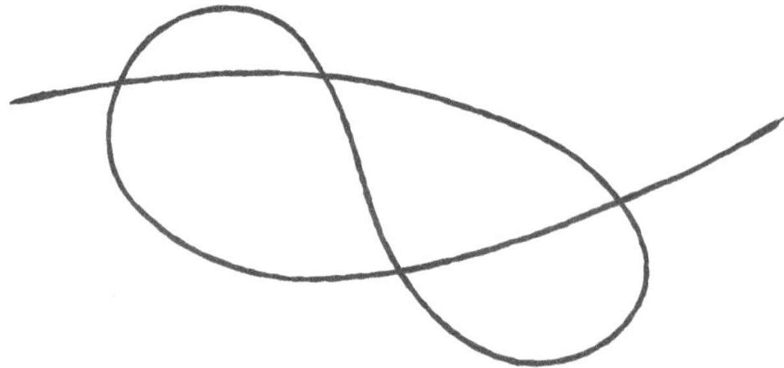

Establishing the Permanence
Section Five

The Permanence is the final stage of the *Brighter Blueprint*, where we secure the edges of the legacy to ensure the mission outlasts our own hands.

The Two Pillars of Systemic Longevity:

To ensure your skyscraper remains standing long after you've left the building, you must master the final two structural disciplines:

Audit the Fraying (Structural Integrity): Even a perfect plan can be unraveled by a single loose thread—an ethical slip, a partisan dig, or personal burnout. Mastery is the ability to perform a *Snag Audit* on your own mission, mending the frays before the system can snap them.

Tie the Final Knot (Succession & Automation): This involves turning your hard-won victories into Standard Operating Procedures (SOPs). You are paving the road so that future families never even encounter the pothole. You move from being the keystone of the arch to the architect of a structure that holds itself up.

Fraying the Tapestry
Blind Spots and Neglect

If you pull a single loose thread on a hand-woven rug, the pattern doesn't disappear immediately. It unravels slowly, a gap opens, and the tension shifts. Eventually, the structural integrity that made the rug useful is lost, leaving you with a pile of useless string.

In advocacy, fraying occurs when we prioritize the skyscraper over the pothole, or when our ego outpaces our integrity.

The Hero Complex

I witnessed this clearly in the aftermath of the Haiti earthquake. The world responded with incredible generosity, but much of that aid was misguided. Organizations rushed in with their own agendas and blueprints devised in air-conditioned offices in D.C. or Geneva, without ever consulting the community members already on the ground.

They provided cold medicine to people who needed clean water and constructed temporary shelters that couldn't withstand the next rainy season. They overlooked the importance of humility and listening. The result? The tapestry frayed because it wasn't woven into the local community. It was merely a patch, not a cohesive weave.

The Chasm of Indifference

We must guard against the chasm of indifference, the space where ignorance and apathy converge. When you see a wrecking ball being taken to institutions you don't fully understand, don't cheer; instead, ask why they exist. Consider what their absence will mean for your life. Fraying occurs when we stop being curious and become certain. To keep the tapestry intact, we must remain in a state of constant curiosity and respect, especially toward those with whom we disagree.

The Three Signs of a Fraying Mission

How can you tell if your own advocacy is starting to unravel? Watch for these three warning signs:

The Echo Chamber: If you only engage with people who already agree with you, your tapestry is becoming a blanket for your own comfort rather than a tool for change. You are no longer learning (**Yellow Thread**); you are just repeating what you believe.

The Celebrity Trap: If the mission focuses more on the advocate than the affected, integrity is lost (**Gray Thread**). If you find yourself more concerned about capturing the perfect selfie during your day at the Capitol than about the details of the legislation, then the thread is snapping.

The Rigidity Snap: If you are so attached to your *Plan A* that you refuse to see alternative paths around obstacles, you will inevitably hit a wall and break (**Purple Thread**). A frayed advocate is a brittle advocate.

When our advocacy frays, it's not just our reputation that suffers; it's the people who are waiting for assistance.

In the rare disease community, a fractured alliance between organizations can stall crucial legislation for a decade. A lack of equity can mean that a life-saving treatment is approved only for families with the right insurance. Every time we fail to interlock our threads, a pothole remains open, and another person falls in.

The Architecture of Systemic Debt

Just as a master weaver must be vigilant for hidden flaws in their yarn, a seasoned advocate must recognize that neglect—whether intentional or accidental—is the greatest threat to systemic change. Advocacy is a system of interdependence. A seemingly minor shortcut or an unexamined ego trap is never truly minor; it is a snag that, under the pressure of a long journey, can unravel the entire work.

In policy, we often discuss technical debt—the cost of choosing an easy, short-term solution today rather than a more effective approach that may take longer. Advocacy operates on the same principle. When you overlook an important thread, you aren't just making a mistake; you are borrowing against your future effectiveness.

This debt is particularly dangerous because it is often invisible until we face high-pressure situations. You might feel like you're progressing faster by skipping learning (**Yellow Thread**) or bypassing listening (**Blue Thread**), but you are actually weakening your mission's structural integrity. When the wind of political change or a regulatory hurdle arrives, a mission burdened with *Systemic Debt* doesn't simply slow down—it can break apart.

Neglecting any single thread leads to *Systemic Debt*. Like an unpaid loan, the interest on this neglect compounds, stalling the mission and exhausting your team. This debt is paid in the most valuable currencies known to an advocate: time, trust, and progress brought to a standstill.

Guarding Against the Unseen Snags

A master weaver doesn't just focus on the front of the tapestry; they are also concerned with the mess on the back. If your mission feels stalled, look for the snag. A snag isn't a failure; it's an early warning.

Thread	The Snag	The Cost
Pink Maintain Resilience	Ignoring rest.	**Engine Failure:** The weaver collapses.
White Practice Humility	Ego over impact.	**Isolation:** Partners exit the room.
Silver Bridge the Divide	Partisan bias.	**Deadlock:** The mission is "benched."
Yellow Learn & Unlearn	Not verifying info.	**Inaccuracy:** Your credibility expires.
Blue Listen for the Unspoken	Guessing at the "Why."	**Miscalculation:** Fixing the wrong problem.
Red Speak with Integrity	Using jargon or "noise."	**Static:** The message is never heard.
Gold Level the Loom	Designing for your own circle	**Unjust Design:** The vulnerable are excluded.
Green Build Alliances	Gatekeeping or solo acts.	**Fragility:** The thread snaps under pressure.
Orange Share the Credit	Hoarding the spotlight	**Resentment:** The "Guild" dissolves.
Gray Lead Ethically	Taking ethical shortcuts	**Firewall Breach:** Trust is permanently lost.
Brown Act Strategically	Ignoring the "potholes."	**Structural Collapse:** No foundation for change.
Purple Master the Pivot	Clinging to a failing plan.	**Obsolescence:** The system moves past you.

Don't try to power through a fraying mission. If the tension is off in the **Blue Thread (Listening)**, adding more **Red Thread (Communication)** will only widen the hole. Identify the moment you chose the skyscraper over the pothole. Did you skip the research? Did you let an ego-trap dictate a meeting? Systemic debt is paid down through transparency. Admit to your partners where the thread was dropped, re-anchor your data, and strengthen the interlock.

Final Mirror Reflections

Pink (Maintain Resilience): Can you name three specific boundaries you have set this month to protect your energy?

White (Practice Humility): If your name were removed from this mission tomorrow, would the work continue, or is the movement built entirely around your personal narrative?

Silver (Bridge the Divide): Can you pitch your solution to the party you *least* align with without using a single partisan buzzword?

Yellow (Learn & Unlearn): If a hostile legislator questioned your data right now, could you cite your source without looking at a screen?

Blue (Listen for the Unspoken): Can you articulate the technical or financial constraints of the person who said "No" better than they can?

Red (Speak with Integrity): Can you explain your ask in sixty seconds to a doctor, a politician, and a grandmother without changing the facts—only the language?

Gold (Level the Loom): Does your solution only work for families with high resources, or does it catch the family in a medical desert?

Gray (Lead Ethically): Where does your personal story end and the systemic data begin? Are you using your trauma as a tool or a crutch?

Green (Build Alliances): Do your closest collaborators all think like you?

If yes, do you have a guild or an echo chamber?

Orange (Share the Credit): When the win happens, is the stage crowded with the partners who pulled the levers, or are you holding the trophy alone?

Brown (Act Strategically): Have you identified the specific administrative rule or bureaucratic step that is actually stalling your progress?

Purple (Master the Pivot): Are you willing to abandon a favorite part of your plan if data shows it is no longer the most effective path?

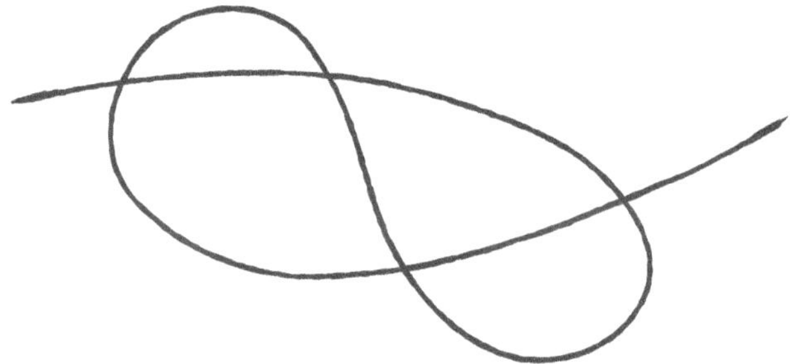

The Final Knot
From Moment to Movement

Background Music: This Is Your Life (Switchfoot)

*Switchfoot's anthem is a wake-up call for the soul. In the **Final Knot**, we stop looking at the past through the lens of "what if" and start looking at the present through "what now." This song captures the moment you realize that your advocacy isn't just a project—it's the life you are choosing to lead. It is the realization that this is the only life you have. What are you waiting for?*

The Full Circle of Resilience

We started the *Brighter Blueprint* with the **Pink Thread**. We talked about the woman in Haiti sweeping her median—the quiet, personal resilience required to show up when everything is in ruins. Now, we come back to that median. But this time, we aren't just sweeping; we are *paving*.

The **Final Knot** is where your internal resilience (the ability to stay in the fight) becomes systemic resilience (the ability of the mission to survive without you). In advocacy, a victory is only a victory if the system cannot easily revert to its broken state once you stop pushing. If you have woven the threads correctly, the knot should feel like a natural conclusion, not a forced ending.

Advocacy is often a lonely craft, practiced in the quiet hours of the night or the sterile halls of a Capitol building where nobody knows your child's name. This blueprint exists so that you never have to guess whether you are making progress. When the world feels chaotic, and the system feels immovable, you can look at your loom and know exactly which thread needs tension.

My journey from Tori's diagnosis to a signed law took exactly **2,292 days.** It was a timeline I couldn't have predicted and a marathon I wasn't prepared to run. In the beginning, I thought advocacy was about the "big moment"—the soaring speech, the stroke of a pen. But as the years went by, I realized that you don't survive a journey that long on passion alone; you survive it through the disciplined application of a proven process.

Passion is the spark that starts the fire, but the *Twelve Threads* are the stones that contain it, ensuring it warms the house instead of burning it down.

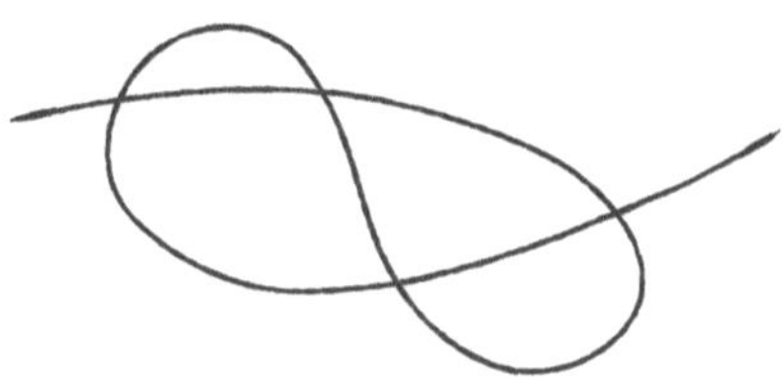

Seeing the Garden

What is a legacy?
It's planting seeds in a garden you never get to see.
Lin-Manuel Miranda (Hamilton)

The tapestry of effective advocacy is never truly finished; it's a continuous, evolving work. Your efforts, combined with those who came before and will come after you, weave a powerful story of collective progress. The fruit of our advocacy is often unseen, and in many ways, that's how it should be. Our work is about planting seeds by serving others, being a voice for the voiceless, and creating a more just and equitable system.

And yet, every once in a while, we get a glimpse of that garden.

The Fruits of Our Labor

When our law went into effect in May 2021, Pennsylvania became the ninth state to screen for Krabbe disease.

Sixty-seven days later, on Tori's birthday, identical twin boys were born and diagnosed with Krabbe disease through newborn screening a week later. They were the first to receive gene therapy for Krabbe disease because of an early diagnosis. They are part of Tori's legacy.

I never expected to meet the children who were diagnosed because of her, but this July, I met three of them, including the twins, Brendan and Trevor. I held them, played with them, and marveled at how well they are doing.

The moment I will truly never forget was when I revealed to their mother who I was and how our stories were intertwined. That hug, those shared tears, are a precious memory for me—two mothers, same disease, but with very different outcomes and a lasting connection.

Newborn screening brings a diagnosis with hope, but it doesn't erase the trauma or pain. We must always acknowledge this in our advocacy.

All we can do is our part to reduce the pain and trauma that comes with any rare diagnosis. Your actions as an advocate are not just about legislative victories; they're about shaping a collective memory for the rare disease community. By sharing your personal story and honoring the work of others, you actively ensure that the lessons, victories, and losses are not forgotten.

Krabbe disease stole so much from our Tori and from us. But our advocacy gives us some peace because we are giving parents something that was taken from us: the opportunity to try to save their child's life. And this is why I continue to advocate, so that no other family has to face the question of **"if only."**

The Blueprint is Complete. The Tapestry Continues.

You now hold all the threads. We have explored the *Brighter Blueprint*—the comprehensive plan for principled action. We have defined the *Twelve Threads* that make up your toolkit, from the wisdom of learning and listening to the power of collaboration and strategic action. You have a framework for communicating your story with integrity, giving credit where it's due, and embracing flexibility when the road gets tough.

The lessons in this book are not just concepts to be understood; they are threads to be woven. The challenges you face as an advocate are unique, but the principles of effective action are universal.

Now, it is your turn. Your tapestry awaits. Your hands may be tired, and the pattern may at times feel too complex to master, but you have the blueprint. The advocacy you create will be unique to your experience, but its strength will come from the universal threads we have explored.

The Brighter Blueprint is complete.

Final Challenge

In one sentence, define the legacy you are weaving for the people who will walk the path after you. *(Example: "I am weaving a world where a diagnosis is a beginning, not an ending.")*

Mirror Reflection

If I walked away from this mission today, would the progress I've made remain, or would it begin to unravel within six months? Am I a load-bearing wall, or am I the architect of a self-supporting structure?

Go fix the potholes. Go build the skyscrapers. The loom is yours.

The Twelve Threads of Effective Advocacy

The Anchor

- **Pink:** Rest isn't quitting. Protecting your peace fuels the mission for the long haul.

- **White:** Humility isn't weakness. Lowering your ego allows you to raise your impact.

- **Silver:** Neutrality isn't a lack of passion. It is the choice to be the bridge that talks to everyone.

The Pattern

- **Yellow:** Expertise isn't elitism. Mastering data is an act of love that keeps your promises.

- **Blue:** Listening isn't passivity. It is a diagnostic tool for sensing the system.

- **Red:** Strategic framing isn't being "fake." It is the respect required to speak so others can hear.

The Weave

- **Gold:** Equity isn't a distraction. It is the quality control that ensures a win for everyone.

- **Green:** Sharing power isn't losing power. A collaborative alliance cannot be snapped.

- **Gray:** Leading with integrity and honesty makes you a permanent, unstoppable force.

The Momentum

- **Orange:** Sharing credit isn't losing status. Shining light on others makes the movement brighter.

- **Brown:** Small wins lead to big change. Fixing potholes builds the road to the mountains.

- **Purple:** Pivoting isn't failing. It is the strategic agility required to survive a changing world.

Epilogue
The Global Tapestry

Background Music: Beautiful Things (Gungor)

In this final movement, we acknowledge that advocacy often begins in the "dust"—the gray dust of Haiti, the orange sand of the Sahara, the literal waste of a landfill, or the sterile dust of a hospital waiting room. This song is the bridge from the rubble of what was lost to the beauty of what is being built. It reminds us that hope isn't just a feeling; it is the evidence of things being re-engineered.

The Ravine: Where the Machinery Fails

In a garbage dump in Chimaltenango, Guatemala, known as *The Ravine*, I saw the ultimate systemic failure. In this place, families survive by scavenging through what the rest of the world has discarded. Some families live on-site, constantly breathing in the smoke from the burning trash. It is a place of literal dust and profound poverty.

But amidst the waste, I met Cesar and Carol.

They didn't have a massive endowment or a political platform. What they had was love and a refusal to look away. They started *The Ravine School* with the conviction that "it doesn't have to be this way."

Because of them, hundreds of children have learned to read, write, and use computers. They are being fed, but more importantly, they are being equipped. Cesar and Carol didn't just build a shelter; they built a **Final Knot.** They created a system—with a local board, local teachers, and community buy-in—that acts as a permanent exit ramp from the cycle of the dump. They stopped fighting the dump and started re-engineering the future of its children.

These beautiful children were given the greatest gift: the ability to *be kids.* To enjoy life. To have a brighter future than their parents and grandparents had. Truly, to make beautiful things out of dust.

The Universal Loom

The blueprint you hold wasn't drafted in a boardroom. It was traced in the gray dust of Port-au-Prince, the crowded souks of Tunisia, and the halls of the Pennsylvania Capitol. Whether you are re-engineering a law or building a school, the structural laws of human impact remain the same:

- **The White Thread (Humility):** We finish the job because we heard the man in the airport say the world never does. We remain students of the struggle.

- **The Brown Thread (Action):** We buy the avocados because we know that solving someone's problem today is the first step toward solving their year. We fix the potholes in front of us.

- **The Purple Thread (Flexibility):** We remain fluid because we know that rigid things eventually snap, but fluidity flows into the cracks to find the way forward.

- **The Gold Thread (Equity):** We design for the median because we know that if the machinery doesn't work for the child in the dust, it doesn't work at all.

I have seen the system fail, and I have seen it rebuilt by people who refused to accept the dust as the final answer. At the Ravine School, the success didn't come from one person wanting to be the savior. It came about because two people were generous enough to build a system that allowed an entire community to own its own future.

Hope as an Engineering Requirement

We can sweep the road knowing it will get dusty again, because the act of sweeping changes us. We can stand in the halls of the Capitol and demand a better blueprint, because we know that hope is a requirement for the build.

The world is big, beautiful, and broken. You don't have to have it all figured out to begin. You just have to be willing to pick up the thread.

I used to think that top-down change was the only way to save the world. I was wrong. The world is saved one thread at a time, by architects who aren't afraid of the dust.

Digital Toolkit

As any artisan knows, a vision without the right tools and materials remains just a dream. That's why we've created *The Brighter Blueprint Studio* and a digital toolkit to support your journey. These resources are designed to be used repeatedly—whether you are on day one or day 2,292 of your mission.

Visit **http://BrighterBlueprint.PatientAdvocacyStrategies.com** or scan the QR code below to access additional resources, including the *Brighter Blueprint Playlist.*

The Rhythm of the Loom
The Brighter Blueprint Playlist

Check out the *Brighter Blueprint* playlist on Spotify!

Introduction	I Saw What I Saw	Sara Groves
Pink	I Still Haven't Found What I'm Looking For	U2
White	Beautiful Day	U2
Silver	On The Turning Away	Pink Floyd
Yellow	The Scientist	Coldplay
Blue	We Can Work It Out	The Beatles
Red	I Won't Back Down	Tom Petty
Gold	Where the Streets Have No Name	U2
Green	Safe and Sound	Capital Cities
Gray	Man in the Mirror	Michael Jackson
Orange	Crowded Table	The Highwomen
Brown	That's The Way It Is	Celine Dion
Purple	I'm Still Standing	Elton John
The Final Knot	This Is Your Life	Switchfoot
Epilogue	Beautiful Things	Gungor
Bonus Tracks	Walk On	U2
	High Hopes	Panic! At the Disco
	Shake it Off	Taylor Swift
	Heal the World	Michael Jackson
	Dare You To Move	Switchfoot
	Meant to Live	Switchfoot
	Say	John Mayer
	Waiting for the World to Change	John Mayer

Acknowledgments

Writing a book about the complexity of advocacy reminds me that no one weaves a tapestry alone. This work reflects a decade of collaboration, shared grief, and collective hope.

To the team at Patient Advocacy Strategies: Thank you for your tireless input, guidance, and technical expertise. You helped me turn years of intuition into a repeatable strategy, and this book is as much a testament to your brilliance as it is to mine.

To Sarah Cortell Vandersypen: Thank you for planting the seed of this book years ago. By asking me to define what it truly meant to be an *effective advocate*, you forced me to move beyond intuition and begin deconstructing the strategy. That invitation was the catalyst for every page that follows.

To my fellow rare disease advocates: You are the "Master Weavers" in the trenches. Thank you for your resilience and for the constant challenge of making a difference despite a system that often resists change. You are proof of what the **Green Thread** can achieve.

To my early readers: Thank you for being willing to read and offer feedback at multiple stages! Your input shaped what the book became, and I cannot thank you enough.

To my husband, Brennan: Thank you for being by my side every step of the way. Through the legislation, the long nights, my crazy ideas, and the life we've built with Isaiah and Caleb, you have been my steady **Pink Thread** of joy and sustainable resilience.

About the Author

Lesa Brackbill is a strategist, mother, and author dedicated to bridging the gap between medical innovation and legislative action. Her journey into advocacy began in 2015 when her daughter, Victoria, was diagnosed with Krabbe Disease—a diagnosis that would lead Lesa and her husband, Brennan, into the heart of the rare disease ecosystem.

Leveraging her background in Political Science and Strategic Communication, Lesa became a key architect of Pennsylvania's Newborn Screening (NBS) reform. Her work led to the enactment of **Act 133 of 2020**, which brought Krabbe screening to the Commonwealth, and **Act 29 of 2022**, a successful coalition effort to expand cCMV screening.

Today, Lesa serves as the **Director of Advocacy for Patient Advocacy Strategies**, where she specializes in building coalitions and educating the next generation of effective advocates. Her influence spans the public and private sectors, including being a board director for **KrabbeConnect.** She is a recognized voice in the technical landscape of screening and serves on various advisory committees.

When she isn't advocating for the world's most vulnerable patients, Lesa serves her local community as a **School Board Director** for the Derry Township School District and shares the legacy of Milton S. Hershey as an historical tour guide at **High Point Mansion.**

Lesa holds a Bachelor of Arts in Political Science and a Master of Arts in Strategic Communication from Azusa Pacific University. She lives in Hershey, PA, with her husband, Brennan, and their identical twin boys, Isaiah and Caleb.

Also by Lesa Brackbill

In *Even So, Joy*, author Lesa Brackbill shares the touching and inspiring story of her first daughter, Victoria, after she was diagnosed with Krabbe disease at only six months old. Despite the tragic circumstances they were dealt, Brennan and Lesa chose joy and life with Tori.

Patient Advocacy Strategies

Patient Advocacy Strategies (PAS) operates at the critical intersection of life sciences innovation and patient insight. We believe that for a medical breakthrough to be truly successful, the patient voice must be more than a checkbox—it must be the foundation upon which the entire clinical and commercial structure is built.

Founded by CEO Mike Walsh and driven by a passionate team, PAS works to harmonize the needs of the biopharma industry with the lived reality of disease communities.

This is the professional home of **The Brighter Blueprint Studio**, where we move beyond theory to operationalize empathy and equity in the boardrooms of global health.

Visit us at: PatientAdvocacyStrategies.com

Endnotes

Preface

1. Grant, A. (2023). *Hidden Potential: The science of achieving greater things*. Viking.

Introduction

1. Hayden, C. (2020, July 19). *Remembering John Lewis: The Power of 'Good Trouble' | Timeless*. The Library of Congress. https://blogs.loc.gov/loc/2020/07/remembering-john-lewis -the-power-of-good-trouble/

Defining Advocacy

1. *What is Advocacy? - Alliance for Justice*. (2023, October 24). Alliance for Justice. https://afj.org/resource/what-is-advocacy/

2. Nguyen, C. Q., Kariyawasam, D., Concepcion, K., Grattan, S., Hetherington, K., Wakefield, C. E., Woolfenden, S., Dale, R. C., Palmer, E., & Farrar, M. A. (2022). 'Advocacy groups are the connectors': Experiences and contributions of rare disease patient organization leaders in advanced neurotherapeutics. Health Expectations, 25(6), 3175–3191. https://doi.org/10.1111/hex.13625

Maintain Resilience

1. Sinek, S. (2009). *Start with Why: How great leaders inspire everyone to take action*. Portfolio/Penguin.

2. Sinek, S. (2010, May 4). *How great leaders inspire action* [Video]. TED Talks. https://www.ted.com/talks/simon_sinek_how_great_leaders_inspire_action

3. Wilson-Mendenhall, C. D., & Dunne, J. D. (2021). Cultivating emotional granularity. *Frontiers in Psychology, 12*, 703658. https://doi.org/10.3389/fpsyg.2021.703658

4. *Labeling our emotions: benefits, neuroscience, and strategies.* (n.d.). https://www.brainfirstinstitute.com/blog/labeling-our-emotions-benefits-neuroscience-and-strategies

5. McMahon, S. (2024). The Small and the Mighty: Twelve Unsung Americans Who Changed the Course of History, from the Founding to the Civil Rights Movement. United States: Penguin Publishing Group.

6. Rock, R. (2020). *One woman can change the world: Reclaiming Your God-Designed Influence and Impact Right Where You Are* (2nd ed.).

7. Edwards, E. (2009). *Resilience: Reflections on the burdens and gifts of facing life's adversities.* Broadway Books.

Practice Humility

1. Ashokkumar, A., Martel, F., Moniz, P., & Swann, W. (2025). Identity fusion and support for political authoritarianism: Lessons from the U.S. insurrection of 2021. Political Psychology, 46(1), 129–143. https://doi.org/10.1111/pops.12979

2. Dalio, R. (2017). *Principles: Life and work.* Avid Reader Press/Simon & Schuster.

Bridge the Divide

1. Brown, B. (2012). *Daring greatly: How the courage to be vulnerable transforms the way we live, love, parent, and lead.* Penguin Random House.

2. Overgaard, C. S. B., Masullo, G. M., Duchovnay, M., & Moore, C. (2022). Theorizing Connective Democracy: a new way to bridge political divides. *Mass Communication & Society, 25*(6), 861–885. https://doi.org/10.1080/15205436.2022.2119870

3. Godin, S. (2018). *This is marketing: You can't be seen until you learn to see.* Portfolio/Penguin.

4. Nichols, T. (2017). *The Death of Expertise: The campaign against established knowledge.* Oxford University Press.

5. Huddy, L., & Bankert, A. (2017, May 24). Political Partisanship as a Social Identity. *Oxford Research Encyclopedia of Politics.* Retrieved 11 Feb. 2026, from https://oxfordre.com/politics/view/10.1093/acrefo re/9780190228637.001.0001/acrefore-9780190228637-e-250.

6. **Haidt, J. (2012). *The Righteous Mind: Why good people are divided by politics and religion.* Vintage. p. 321**

7. TEDx Talks. (2019, February 1). *The dark side of our personal marketing data | Kirk Grogan | TEDxSeattle* [Video]. YouTube. https://www.youtube.com/watch?v=wIxQF0-6oPs

8. *Bail, C.A., et al. (2018).* "Exposure to opposing views on social media can increase political polarization." *PNAS.*

9. *List of Cognitive Biases and Heuristics - The Decision Lab.* (2024, May 27). The Decision Lab. https://thedecisionlab.com/biases/belief-pe rseverance

10. Cinelli, M., Morales, G. D. F., Galeazzi, A., Quattrociocchi, W., & Starnini, M. (2021). The echo chamber effect on social media. *Proceedings of the National Academy of Sciences of the United States of America, 118*(9).

11. Garimella, K., De Francisci Morales, G., Gionis, A., & Mathioudakis, M. (2018, April). Political discourse on social media: Echo chambers, gatekeepers, and the price of bipartisanship. In *Proceedings of the 2018 World Wide Web Conference* (pp. 913-922).

12. Del Vicario, M., Bessi, A., Zollo, F., Petroni, F., Scala, A., Caldarelli, G., ... & Quattrociocchi, W. (2016). The spreading of misinformation online. *Proceedings of the National Academy of Sciences, 113*(3), 554–559

13. Overgaard, C. S. B., Masullo, G. M., Duchovnay, M., & Moore, C. (2022). Theorizing Connective Democracy: a new way to bridge political divides. *Mass Communication & Society, 25*(6), 861–885. https://doi.org/10.1080/15205436.2022.2119870

14. Misch, A., Fergusson, G., & Dunham, Y. (2018). Temporal dynamics of partisan identity fusion and prosociality during the 2016 U.S. Presidential Election. *Self and Identity, 17*(5), 531–548. https://doi.org/10.1080/15298868.2018.1430063

15. Brown, B. (2018, May 17). *Dehumanizing always starts with language.* https://brenebrown.com/articles/2018/05/17/dehumanizing-always-starts-with-language/

16. McKnight, S. (2022, November 29). Stories work. *Scot's Newsletter.* https://scotmcknight.substack.com/p/stories-work?r=13tul&utm_campaign=post&utm_medium=web&fbclid=IwAR2V-75zqLqJiFcESyzkiIkWU4NQtdXEDm_rhTRoSEaP8hZvF9owvFwfV4A

17. Noëlle-Neumann, E. (1974). "The spiral of silence: A theory of public opinion." *Journal of Communication.*

18. Haile, Y. A. (2022). "The theoretical wedding of spiral of silence and echo chambers." *The Journal of Communication and Media Studies.*

19. Wardell, A., PhD. (2026, February 10). How teaching changed what I think about advocacy. *Psychology Today.* https://www.psychologytoday.com/us/blog/compassionate-feminism/202602/fostering-change-moving-from-influence-to-impact

20. Masullo, G. M., Lu, S., & Fadnis, D. (2020). Does online incivility cancel out the spiral of silence? A moderated mediation model of willingness to speak out. *New Media & Society, 23*(11), 3391-3414. https://doi.org/10.1177/1461444820954194 (Original work published 2021)

Learn and Unlearn

1. Ling, R. (2020). Confirmation Bias in the Era of Mobile News Consumption: The Social and Psychological Dimensions. *Digital Journalism, 8*(5), 596–604. https://doi.org/10.1080/21670811.2020.1766987

2. Grant, A. (2021). *Think again: The power of knowing what you don't know.* Viking.

Listen for the Unspoken

1. Itzchakov, G., Weinstein, N., Leary, M., Saluk, D., & Amar, M. (2024). Listening to understand: The role of high-quality listening on speakers' attitude depolarization during disagreements. *Journal of personality and social psychology, 126*(2), 213–239. https://doi.org/10.1037/pspa0000366

2. Bilanich, B. (2017, July 6). *Success common sense: Listen to understand not to criticize others' point of view*. Retrieved October 7, 2023, from https://www.proquest.com/blogs-podcasts-websites/success-comm on-sense-listen-understand-not/docview/1916492326/se-2?accoun tid=8459

3. Guzmán, M. (2022). *I never thought of it that way: How to have fearlessly curious conversations in dangerously divided times*. BenBella Books.

4. Itzchakov, G., PhD. (2025, December 17). Why Carl Rogers, the "father" of active listening would hate how it's used today. *Psychology Today*. https://www.psychologytoday.com/us/blog/the-listening-l ens/202512/the-problem-with-active-listening

5. Guzman's book powerfully demonstrates this concept.

6. Overgaard, C. S. B., Masullo, G. M., Duchovnay, M., & Moore, C. (2022). Theorizing Connective Democracy: a new way to bridge political divides. *Mass Communication & Society*, *25*(6), 861–885. https://doi.org/10.1080/15205436.2022.2119870

7. Overgaard, G. M. M. a. C. S. B. (n.d.). *Connective Democracy: A New Way of Thinking about Deliberative Democra*. Media Ethics Magazine. https://www.mediaethicsmagazine.com/index.php/browse-back-is sues/216-spring-2021-vol-32-no-2/3999346-connective-democra cy-a-new-way-of-thinking-about-deliberative-democracy

8. Murphy, K. (2020). *You're Not Listening: What you're missing and why it matters*. Celadon Books. (p 38)

9. Murphy, 88.

10. Chong, D., & Druckman, J. N. (2007). Framing theory. *Annual Review of Political Science, 10*(1), 103–126. https://doi.org/10.1146/annurev.polisci.10.072805.103054

11. Fisher, W. R. (1985). The narrative paradigm: in the beginning. *Journal of Communication, 35*(4), 74–89. https://doi.org/10.1111/j.1460-2466.1985.tb02974.x

12. Grunig, J. E (1997). A situational theory of publics: Conceptual history, recent challenges and   new research. *D., Moss, T., MacMannus, & D., Vercic (Eds). Public relations research: An international perspective,* 3-48.

13. Ramos Salazar, L. (2017). "Changing resistant audience attitudes using social judgment theory's 'anchor' point perspectives." *Communication Teacher.*

14. Sarup, G., Suchner, R. W., & Gaylord, G. (1991). Contrast Effects and Attitude Change: A Test of the Two-Stage Hypothesis of Social Judgment Theory. Social Psychology Quarterly, 54(4), 364–372. https://doi.org/10.2307/2786848

15. McCombs, M. E., Shaw, D. L., & Weaver, D. H. (2014). New Directions in Agenda-Setting Theory and Research. *Mass Communication and Society, 17*(6), 781–802. https://doi.org/10.1080/15205436.2014.964871

16. Almaney, A. (1974). Communication and the Systems Theory of Organization. *Journal of Business Communication, 12*(1), 35–43. https://doi.org/10.1177/002194367401200106

17. *3 Lenses for Management Success | MIT Sloan.* (2014, March 10). MIT Sloan. https://mitsloan.mit.edu/emba/3-lenses-management-success

18. Itzchakov, G., PhD. (2025, December 17). Why Carl Rogers, the "father" of active listening would hate how it's used today. *Psychology Today*. https://www.psychologytoday.com/us/blog/the-listening-lens/202512/the-problem-with-active-listening

19. Guzmán, M. (2022). *I never thought of it that way: How to have fearlessly curious conversations in dangerously divided times*. BenBella Books.

Speak with Integrity

1. Brown, B. (2010, December 23). *The power of vulnerability* [Video]. TED Talks. https://www.ted.com/talks/brene_brown_the_power_of_vulnerability

2. Liu, J., Su, M., McLeod, D. M., Abisaid, J., & Lu, L. (2020). The effects of framing and advocacy expectancy on belief importance and issue attitude. Mass Communication and Society, 23(4), 537–553. https://doi.org/10.1080/15205436.2020.1728776

Level the Loom

1. *Life Expectancy: Could where you live influence how long you live?* (2025, October 15). RWJF. https://www.rwjf.org/en/insights/our-research/interactives/whereyouliveaffectshowlongyoulive.html

2. Blackwell, A. G. (n.d.). *The Curb-Cut effect (SSIR)*. (C) 2005-2026. https://ssir.org/articles/entry/the_curb_cut_effect

3. *What is Universal Design? – The UD Project*. (n.d.). The UD Project. https://universaldesign.org/definition

Forge Alliances

1. Mahajan, R., Lim, W. M., Sareen, M., Kumar, S., & Panwar, R. (2023). Stakeholder theory. *Journal of Business Research, 166,* 114104. https://doi.org/10.1016/j.jbusres.2023.114104

2. Grant, A. (2023). *Hidden potential: The science of achieving greater things.* Viking.

3. Covey, S. R. (1989). *The 7 habits of highly effective people: Restoring the character ethic.* Simon & Schuster.

4. Godoy, M. (2018, January 15). Meet the fearless cook who secretly fed — and funded — the civil rights movement. *NPR.* https://www.npr.org/sections/thesalt/2018/01/15/577675950/meet -the-fearless-cook-who-secretly-fed-and-funded-the-civil-rights -movement

5. Freeman, R. E. (2010). *Strategic management: A stakeholder approach.* Cambridge university press.

Lead Ethically

1. Umeogu, B. (2012). Source Credibility: A philosophical analysis. *Open Journal of Philosophy, 02*(02), 112–115. https://doi.org/10.423 6/ojpp.2012.22017

Share the Credit

1. Nickerson, C. (2023, October 25). *Social Exchange Theory of Relationships: Examples & More.* Simply Psychology. https://www.simp lypsychology.org/what-is-social-exchange-theory.html

2. May, C. R., Mair, F., Finch, T., MacFarlane, A., Dowrick, C., Treweek, S., Rapley, T., Ballini, L., Ong, B. N., Rogers, A., Murray, E., Elwyn, G., Légaré, F., Gunn, J., & Montori, V. M. (2009). Development of a theory of implementation and integration: Normalization Process Theory. *Implementation Science*, 4(1), 29. https://doi.org/10.1186/1748-5908-4-29

3. Doyle, B. (2019). *One long river of song: Notes on wonder*. Little, Brown and Company.

Calibrating the Guild

1. Oliver, M. (2017). The summer day. In *Devotions: The selected poems of Mary Oliver* (p. 154). Penguin Press. (Original work published 1992)

Act Strategically

1. *Incrementalism | Social Sciences and Humanities | Research Starters | EBSCO Research.* (n.d.). EBSCO. https://www.ebsco.com/research-starters/social-sciences-and-humanities/incrementalism

2. *PDSA cycle - The W. Edwards Deming Institute.* (n.d.). The W. Edwards Deming Institute. https://deming.org/explore/pdsa/

3. *Circling back | ASQ.* (n.d.). https://asq.org/quality-progress/articles/circling-back?id=5e4d20950fad4b519133490466ccbf0a https://deming.org/wp-content/uploads/2020/06/circling-back.pdf

4. Doran, G.T. (1981) There's a SMART Way to Write Management's Goals and Objectives. Journal of Management Review, 70, 35-36. https://community.mis.temple.edu/mis0855002fall2015/files/2015/10/S.M.A.R.T-Way-Management-Review.pdf

Master the Pivot

1. *How the Sunk Cost Fallacy Can Drive Bad Decisions*. (n.d.). Greater Good. https://greatergood.berkeley.edu/article/item/how_the_sunk_cost_fallacy_can_drive_bad_decisions

2. *The sunk cost fallacy*. (2024, September 6). The Decision Lab. Retrieved February 4, 2026, from https://thedecisionlab.com/biases/the-sunk-cost-fallacy